St Nazaire
Commando

St Nazaire
Commando

Stuart Chant-Sempill
OBE MC

PRESIDIO

Copyright © 1985 by Stuart Chant-Sempill
First published 1985
by John Murray (Publishers) Ltd
50 Albemarle Street, London W1X 4BD

First published in the United States 1987
by Presidio Press
31 Pamaron Way, Novato CA 94949

Library of Congress Cataloging-in-Publication Data

Chant-Sempill, Stuart.
    St. Nazaire commando.

    Bibliography: p. 200
    Includes index.
    1. World War, 1939-1945--France--St. Nazaire.
2. World War, 1939-1945--Commando operations--France--
St. Nazaire. 3. Docks--France--St. Nazaire--History--
20th century. 4. Saint-Nazaire (France)--History.
I. Title.   II. Title: Saint Nazaire commando.
D762.S26C48   1987   940.54'21   87-12540
ISBN 0-89141-315-4

Printed in the United States of America

Contents

Contents

Illustrations

SOURCES OF ILLUSTRATIONS

1, 2, 17, 18, 19, 20: the Author; 3, 8, 9, 10, 16: Camera Press, London; 4: Mrs M. Barling; 5, 15, 21–5: Imperial War Museum, London; 6, 7: Captain R. E. D. Ryder VC; 11: Popperfoto, London; 12, 13, 14: Bilderdienst Süddeutscher Verlag, Munich

To all who died at St Nazaire
on 28 March 1942
and every Commando since

Acknowledgements

The attack on St Nazaire was not just a Commando raid. It was an operation of high strategy, and was an important part of the Battle of the Atlantic. For St Nazaire boasted the largest dry-dock in the world, the destruction of which was vital if Germany's battleships, pocket battleships and heavy cruisers were to be denied the safe refuge it then provided from attack.

In the words of Admiral of the Fleet, Sir Charles Forbes: '. . . this operation was badly reported (both at the time and subsequently) and also, owing to good German propaganda, many people (both here and abroad) were led to believe that the raid had not been a success'. As the Admiral further reported, the high cost in dead and of those who were taken prisoner prevented a true chronicle of events being pieced together until after the war ended. It was a success, however, and the Germans' capital ships never ventured into the Atlantic Ocean again, and were subsequently destroyed at their anchor chains and moorings whilst hiding in Norwegian fjords.

When I started this book, a few years ago, I could not write as I had just lost the power in my right hand and had to learn to write with my other hand. After months of scrawling on large sheets of foolscap paper, my book took shape and includes an eyewitness account of events leading up to, during and after the attack on St Nazaire.

In attempting to recall events of those days I had the benefit of the short and authoritative book by Captain R. E. D. Ryder VC RN, our force Commander; and the excellent account by the late Brigadier C. E. Lucas Phillips who stuck his label 'The Greatest Raid of All' on to the chain of events.

Acknowledging the direct help I received at this time I have to pay special thanks to Major E. F. D. (David) Campbell MC, who generously let me quote from his personal unpublished account of our prisoner-of-war lives and of a major escape attempt which forms an important part of the book. I was also greatly assisted by friendly ladies who patiently transcribed my 'scrawl' to type, in particular to Mrs Edward Fife, widow of 'Ed', an American top executive, of Lockheed Aircraft Corporation, and with whom I worked for a brief period. Also to Miss Jann Grant, who typed my final manuscript and whom I met through the patient and expert Miss Mary Griffith, a professional editor who finally introduced me to my publisher and who has done so much to encourage me.

I am grateful to George Greenfield, Chairman of John Farquharson Ltd, who gave me advice based on his experience and wisdom as a literary agent; to the staff of the Public Record Office in Kew; to the staff of the Imperial War Museum; to comrades still living who were at St Nazaire with me, particularly Captain Ryder VC who helped me with his own photographs; Lord Newborough DSC (then Sub-Lieutenant 'Micky' Wynn); Lt-Colonel 'Bob' Montgomery MC; Frank Carr DSM; 'Dick' Bradley MM; A.C. 'Alf' Searson MM; Eric de la Torre; Robbie Barron; John A. May; Henry Brown, Secretary of the Commando Association; Associated British Ports; and last and by no means least, my wife, who patiently bore with my frustrations, and at being awoken at 5.30 every morning so I could write down these memories, before going off to my office in the City.

Foreword

by Lord Lovat DSO MC

St Nazaire was unquestionably the most spectacular sea-borne raid carried out in the Second World War. Except for similar heroism shown by an earlier generation at Zeebrugge there is no comparable operation in which a small force successfully carried its main objective despite heavy casualties, and then went on to wreck defended harbour installations and win five Victoria Crosses before mostly being sunk, killed, or captured by the enemy.

I remember the author, Stuart Chant* – who distinguished himself that night by blowing up the giant pumping-station – as a dashing Officer in the Gordon Highlanders; he had turned into a demolitionist for this important occasion, armed with high explosives.

Stuart was an early volunteer for Commando service during the formative period required to create our special combined operational set-up, then a new name on the army list, not altogether popular, but destined to become – thanks to men like Stuart Chant – very definitely a *corps d'élite*.

After the humiliating defeats of our armies both in France and Norway Churchill called for a new type of soldier to take the fight back to the enemy in occupied Europe:

> I feel that the Germans have been right in both wars in what use they have made of stormtroops. The defeat of France was accomplished by a small number of highly equipped and brilliantly led spearheads. There will be many opportunities for surprise landings by nimble forces accustomed to work like packs of hounds instead of being moved about in the ponderous

* Now Stuart Chant-Sempill, by decree of the Lyon Court, 1966.

manner which is appropriate for regular formations: for every reason, therefore, we must develop the stormtroop or Commando idea. I have asked for five thousand of these 'bands of brothers' capable of lightning action.

The response was immediate and volunteers poured in. They were not supermen – far from it – but certain things were expected from them and, with patience, they grew in stature for they were superbly trained.

Stuart passed with a good mark through the Irregular Warfare School at Lochailort in the western Highlands (forty-five years ago I served there as an instructor on the Field Craft Wing); he had already fought a rearguard action across Belgium and France with the BEF, returning to England by way of Dunkirk. It is not surprising that after a further course at Lochailort he was hand-picked by Colonel Newman of No 2 Commando to train in a new role for the St Nazaire raid.

This is a vivid story told with modesty by a brave man who, after being crippled by wounds during the battle, was picked up, when his legs gave out, by a German patrol and put in the 'bag' to endure two years of suffering and hardship as a prisoner-of-war. Reading between the lines which describe this experience – written in simple language without frills, that might have crept in after the lapse of time – I am astonished by the self-discipline and forbearance shown by a man who was seldom out of pain during that close confinement. There are some grim asides: the frequent operations in prison hospitals without the benefit of drugs or anaesthetics make the blood run cold: yet German doctors and camp officials, however stern or brutal, are described dispassionately as men who did their duty – according to their lights.

By way of contrast there is a touching reference to kindness shown by the giant hospital orderly from Senegal, himself a half-starved prisoner, who tenderly nursed the author through his darkest hours. I suspect there must have been mutual respect on both sides involved. He touches briefly on the sense of despair that came from lying 'incommunicado' for months in hospital, lost and out of touch with the world beyond the gates. But the author never let his guard down, and there is no trace of bitterness.

Stuart has told what was expected from Commandos and what manner of men they were. But no praise is too high for the Royal Navy who got them to their destination, or for the boat officers and ratings who fought alongside. Commander Ryder RN, and Lt-Commander Beattie RN (on *Campbeltown*) and Able Seaman Savage, who died of wounds on Ryder's gunboat, all won the Victoria Cross, and are legendary heroes who will surely be remembered. Enough has been written to give an idea of the actual assault on St Nazaire in a scene that is difficult to describe amid the pandemonium of a night attack. For those who got ashore – confused fighting raged round the buildings on the docks, both sides shooting it out at point-blank range. Street fighting in built-up areas at night is never pleasant. In darkness, the tossed hand-grenade, sudden confrontation round corners, and the richochets off walls that kill men by mistake, are difficult to deal with.

Few of that gallant company survived to return down river. The cost of the raid included 169 officers and men killed; 200 wounded and captured; four out of nineteen vessels survived and returned to England. Of those who were left behind, five unwounded men escaped capture. These walked across France to the Spanish frontier, climbed the Pyrenees, and eventually got back to England from the Mediterranean.

What lay behind Operation CHARIOT? And why take such desperate risks? There were good reasons. In 1941/2 German U-boats as well as enemy surface craft were sinking our supply ships faster than we could replace them. On the west coast of France 300 miles from our nearest harbour, Falmouth, stands the port of St Nazaire where the River Loire runs into the sea. The fact that it possessed the only dry-dock on the Atlantic seaboard capable of holding the German battleship *Tirpitz* made it of vital importance to the enemy.

It was to this haven that *Bismarck* was undoubtedly making

when she was sunk in the previous summer. But *Tirpitz*, her sister ship, was still at sea and it had been learned through Intelligence sources in spring 1942 that this battleship, then in Norwegian waters, was preparing to enter the Atlantic.

Once there, the damage she might cause our shipping lanes would be incalculable. The dry-dock facilities in France *had* to be shut against her.

Introduction

The 600 British soldiers of the Light Brigade who charged the Russian guns in the Crimea in 1854, and earned themselves immortal fame, were not mad, even though their commanding general, Lord Cardigan, undoubtedly was. The 600 men who charged the German guns at St Nazaire on 28 March 1942 were certainly not mad either, nor were their joint commanding officers, respectively a sailor and a soldier. They were highly professional and they operated a plan so detailed and complex that it shook the German High Command's sense of superiority out of its complacency.

That raid on St Nazaire has been described as 'the greatest raid of all' notably by Brigadier C.E. Lucas Phillips in his book, published in 1958, which used that very title. But the only one of us who took part in the raid, and who has offered a published account of it, is Commander (later Captain) R.E.D. Ryder, in his book *The Raid on St Nazaire* (1947). However his account, as one would expect, was confined largely to describing the naval operations of the action for, apart from brief references to the fighting on shore, he had no first-hand knowledge of what took place there other than through embarking several of the wounded during the fighting. Not one of us who was actually landed at St Nazaire, and took part in the fighting and the demolitions, has yet attempted to describe in writing what took place. We who survived have, of course, been interviewed by professional writers and historians, and they have produced accurate descriptions of the raid; but there are still aspects of the action which have never been recorded.

There is a reason: many sailors and soldiers were killed at the time and, as in any other battle, many died doing their duty, but with no one to witness their successes and sacrifices. Here, perhaps, I was luckier than most, because I was fortunate enough to be repatriated in the first repatriation party of the war, and, as it transpired, I was the first army officer captured at St Nazaire to be returned to Britain. There was, admittedly, a handful of soldiers who escaped directly the action was finished but, precisely because of that, they had no means of checking with each other as to what had actually happened to the rest of us. Indeed, when Admiral Sir Charles Forbes, the Commander-in-Chief, Plymouth, wrote his report on Operation CHARIOT, as it was called, after the raid he was obliged to confess that there was little in it about 'the admirable work of the Commando troops because, unfortunately, none who took part has returned'.

SC-S

London and Aberdeenshire
1985

I

Commando

Before the Second World War I was a 'Blue Button' on the floor of the London Stock Exchange. My main outside interest was Rugby football and I played for the old club Wasps in every one of their ten teams from the Extra C XV to the 1st XV – and on Sundays 'illegally' for the Sudbury Stallions (Sudbury was the Wasps' ground), a side of players made up from the Wasps and the exiles' sides – London Welsh, London Scottish and London Irish – mixed with players of international fame.

At that time I was also a private soldier in the Artists' Rifles, a regiment with honours from the South African war, and in the First World War. Having trained for the war which we 'knew' would come after the false alarm of Munich in 1938, I was commissioned with others in October 1939, a month after the outbreak of hostilities.

I was lucky enough to escape with the British Expeditionary Force from Dunkirk from the beach at Bray Dunes – I waded out to a small boat and thence to a small coaster to sail away to Ramsgate, arriving back in England on 31 May 1940. Then I was sent to re-form at Oxford.

Shortly after our return to England an order was circulated seeking volunteers for 'special service'. Certain qualifications were listed: an ability to march long distances – I reckoned I must have marched hundreds of miles in my three-and-a-half years' service in the Artists' Rifles; the ability to swim, which I could, well; and a knowledge of small boats – I used to spend weekends sailing and fishing at sea. I applied and, in October 1940, was accepted and ordered to join No 5 Commando, then stationed in Felixstowe.

For the next two years we trained and trained, mostly in

Scotland where we were sent: to Helensburgh on the banks of the Clyde, to Inverary to live on board ship, and to the western Highlands for special and extra intensive training. Later we were shipped to Falmouth and then Dartmouth, and it was there that my story began to crystallise into 'action'.

In February 1942 I was stationed with No 5 Commando in Dartmouth, Devon, and, as was normal practice in our training, I was periodically sent with a small group of officers and NCOs to the north of Scotland for further instruction. There, at Inverailort Castle, Lochailort, on 'The Road to the Isles' in the western Highlands, I reported – for the third time in two years – at the Irregular Warfare Special Training Centre where the original Commandos had been training since 1940.

Strangely, little has been written about Lochailort. While Achnacarry, or 'Castle Commando', has often been described as the place where Commandos were trained, it did not exist as a training centre until 1942. Until then, it was at Lochailort that we first learnt the rudiments and refinements of Commando life.

Inverailort is not very old compared with other castles in Scotland, where some keeps and towers go back to the fourteenth and fifteenth centuries. It is large, draughty and rather grim-looking, and it stands on the shores of Lochailort, overshadowed by a mountain called An Stac, 2350 ft high. Not many people live in the area and its very seclusion was a natural screen for our activities. In fact the whole of that part of Scotland was a 'restricted area' during the war; security was close and the district was guarded from the eyes of the curious would-be observer.

It used to be an axiom in the war: 'Never volunteer – your number will come up all in good time – meanwhile, keep your head down.' But after the bitter defeats the British suffered in Norway, Belgium and France in 1940, and the creation of the 'special service' a new word began to enter army language. The word originated in the Boer War when the Dutch Afrikaners fought the British army with their fast mobile sections of farmer-soldiers, all too often bringing the slow-moving mass of the British infantry to a standstill. These sections were called by their Dutch (and German) name Kommandos, and it was the memory of those successful Boer principles of speed, mobility and surprise which inspired Winston Churchill, now Prime Minister, from his own Boer War experience, to form special units of a similar nature and give them the name of Commandos.

Admiral of the Fleet (Sir Roger) Lord Keyes was the 'father' of the Commandos but the man who actually invented the British Commandos was Lt-Colonel Dudley Clarke who, having grown up in the Transvaal, had had the same idea as the Prime Minister, and because he was Military Assistant to Sir John Dill, the Chief of Imperial General Staff, through him had direct access to Churchill.

Today it seems as though nearly every country in the world operates such Commando units, but it was that call for volunteers in 1940 which seemed to revive the ancient and basic military principles which had been so sadly lacking before the evacuation from Dunkirk.

By the early autumn of 1940 twelve Commandos had been formed, each consisting of twenty-five officers and 460 men. The units purposely had little administrative tail, for each man was taught to live off the land. This was fundamental to the whole idea and to the hard training which followed; and those men who could not last the course or the pace of events were politely returned to their units – RTU, a horrid but inescapable label of failure.

The training, therefore, was aimed at producing self-sufficiency: every man had to be able to swim; since the units had no transport, they had to march long distances, non-stop; and very fast over short distances. The standards set for all ranks were 60 miles in 24 hours, and 7 miles in the hour – almost twice the speed of the standard infantryman. Tests were carried out at regular intervals of a month; on one occasion my own troop

covered 64 miles in 23 hours, from the far northern edge of
Bodmin Moor in Cornwall to Falmouth in the south. We were
to repeat the training later in Scotland. Everyone had to take
turns in carrying the heavier weapons such as Bren guns and the
cumbersome Boys anti-tank rifle – often breaking them down
into their component parts and sharing the weight between all
ranks. We were also initiated into the skills of handling explosives, demolition and unarmed combat.

Among the instructors at Lochailort were officers and men
with peacetime experience of hardship in the Antarctic and
Arctic and of the recent fighting in Norway, France and
Belgium. One of these had been with Captain Scott on his
historic expedition to the Antarctic in 1910-13: Surgeon-
Commander Murray Levick, RN.

Lord Lovat, himself later to become one of the most famous
Commando soldiers of the war, was also at Lochailort with
NCOs from his family regiment, The Lovat Scouts, keepers
and ghillies who knew the mountains better than anyone. They
had lived all their lives in the Highlands, could walk all day
without rest, and climb their mountains and look after themselves in the open in all weathers.

When I first reported there as a student in 1941, the Colonel
of Lochailort was a regular soldier from the Royal Welch
Fusiliers – a veritable fire-eater – who had survived the fighting
in Norway, was already highly decorated, and later commanded
a Division in the Burma jungle: Lt-Colonel 'Hughie' Stockwell,
DSO*.

There were others of equal ability and distinction, such as
Captains Sykes and Fairburn, two ex-policemen from the
Shanghai Police Force, who instructed us in the gentlemanly art
of unarmed combat; Major Jim Gavin, who had been on the
1936 Everest expedition. There were others experienced in
exploration, mountaineering and endurance in the years before
the war – Andrew Croft (later Colonel, DSO, OBE) who was an

---

* Now General Sir Hugh Stockwell.

Arctic explorer and author of the book *Polar Exploration*; David Stirling of No 8 Commando and later of the SAS.

Each course lasted several weeks and the students, whether officers or NCOs, were all treated as equals and were instructed in the art of survival in the cold and snow of a Highland winter. The courses were later extended to include the majority of Commando soldiers so that nearly every Commando, troop by troop, sixty men at a time, went to Lochailort.

These Commando courses always culminated in a three-day-and-night-long test of endurance and, sadly, there were some fatal casualties from our exposure to the elements of those Highland winters. Each man, whether officer or soldier, had to fend for himself and prepare his own food from the meagre rations of oatmeal, chocolate, cocoa and tea which were issued to him. In order to maintain interest, we marched over the historic trails of the clans and, in particular, I remember the march we made along the dark slopes of Loch Morar, following the steps of Bonnie Prince Charlie as he made his escape after the defeat at Culloden in 1745.

The impact on us of this specialist training and of these feats of endurance was extraordinary. Even the humblest and smallest soldier quickly developed into a man 'twice his height', as it were, who thought nothing of hardships which would have seemed impossible to him and his mates a few weeks before arriving in that lonely part of Scotland. It was this development which eventually resulted in the establishment of the Commando Training Centre at Achnacarry in 1942, the home of Cameron of Lochiel, which became known, rightly or wrongly, as 'Castle Commando'.

In addition to attaining peak physical fitness all Commando soldiers and officers were taught how to man small boats and lend a hand on naval ships. During 1940-1 nearly all Commandos were stationed in Scotland and we spent several weeks at sea on ships such as HMT *Ettrick* and *Karanja*, both ex-BI liners, with the other Commandos – Royal Marine battalions and Guards regiments. For at that time we formed part of General

Sir Harold (later Lord) Alexander's '110' Force standing by to land in the Mediterranean, probably Pantelleria near Sicily.

In 1941, however, after No 5 Commando was moved from Helensburgh on the Clyde to Cornwall, there was no shelter from German air attacks for the large troop carriers and support vessels on which we had trained in the lochs of western Scotland. So we requisitioned several small vessels for a continuation of our sea training from Falmouth Docks. Then a seemingly heaven-sent opportunity presented itself in the fleet of refugee fishing vessels which had escaped from Belgian ports when Belgium was overrun in 1940. These had eventually found safe haven in the small fishing ports along the southwest coast of England, particularly Newlyn in Cornwall. There the Belgians had settled down and carried on fishing, for the English market, until they were bombed and strafed by the Luftwaffe, and lost a number of vessels and crew members. The Belgians then refused to fish any more unless they were given protection by the Royal Navy. But the Navy had no vessels to spare for such seemingly mundane duties.

Thus arose the idea of giving to each fishing vessel two or three Commando soldiers, each one manning a Bren or a stripped Lewis gun.

There were approximately a score of vessels at Newlyn and they fished nearly every day, way out in the Channel, sometimes far too close to the French coast for our liking. They kept together as much as possible, and with our Commando firepower they enjoyed the protection of about sixty machine-guns.

One overcast day a Heinkel 111 bomber flew lazily out of the clouds towards the fishing fleet, presumably intent on destruction. But as the aircraft dived down towards the little boats it suddenly became the target of streams of tracer bullets firing from all sixty guns. Taken by surprise, the plane shuddered, caught fire and exploded, to loud cheers from both Belgian fishermen and British soldiers. In the days that followed there were other attacks, but the Germans soon realised the danger of flying too close to our guns and they kept well out of machine-gun range as they dropped their bombs with negative results.

The Belgians, reassured, continued to fish throughout the summer. Our Commandos, troop by troop, became part-fishermen, part-sailors in addition to continuing their special military training.

We grew so confident that it was even suggested we might keep a watch-out for E-boats in the hope that, if we did encounter one, we would wait for the enemy vessel to come alongside and then attack it with a hail of grenades and kill everyone in sight with our machine-guns! But in spite of continuous patrols we had no luck – we were too far down the Channel and, in any event, the fishermen were not very enthusiastic. Aircraft were hazard enough; E-boats were something else.

However, although we were very proud of our fitness, we were at that stage doing nothing more than had already been learnt in the centuries of soldiering before and particularly during the days of Wellington, Moore and the horrors of trench warfare in 1914-18. No specific tasks had yet been laid at our door, although some raids had been successfully carried out against the Germans, particularly in the Lofoten Islands and at Vaagso the year before.

2

Highly Intensive Training

It was after two visits to the North – to 'Hell's Glen' as we now dubbed Lochailort – that in early spring 1942 I was once again deposited on the platform of that remote station and made to run the two miles all the way to Inverailort Castle with the other soldier passengers. Once again we were living there in the cold Nissen huts scattered amongst the shrubs and rhododendron bushes in the grounds of the castle. Once again we were paraded each morning in the half-light of winter.

But this time there was a difference: instead of the physical training and tests of endurance we were now being initiated into the handling of more sophisticated explosives and destruction than hitherto. We enjoyed blowing up dead trees and large slabs of mountainside, but it did not cross our minds that this portended our being earmarked for duties of a different kind; and after weeks of this training we returned to our respective Commandos around the coasts of Scotland and England. With two other officers and twelve NCOs I returned to No 5 Commando in Dartmouth; but the only memorable incident of those days was being paraded for inspection by the new leader of Combined Operations, Admiral Lord Louis Mountbatten, who had just been promoted to Rear-Admiral after fighting his destroyer with great courage in the North Sea and then during the fighting off Crete when his famous ship, HMS *Kelly*, was bombed and sunk. Admiral Sir Roger Keyes was the first commander of Combined Operations and did great work in setting up the whole operation in 1940: Lord Louis inspected us at the Royal Naval College, Dartmouth, where we were doing much of our indoor training and instruction.

However, soon after this, we, the Lochailort party, were on the move north once again. On the long train journey to Scotland we wondered why – Lochailort, yet again? No. This time we detrained at Edinburgh and arrived in Burntisland, a small port on the northern bank of the Firth of Forth in the Kingdom of Fife. There, we met friends from the other Commandos (Nos 1, 2, 3, 4, 6, 9 and 12) who had been with us at Lochailort. We were still uncertain, however. Was this the real thing at last or yet another practice?

At Burntisland we were also joined by a good-looking young captain from the Special Service Brigade. Captain W.H. 'Bill' Pritchard of the Royal Engineers, a demolition and explosives expert, was to be our instructor. He had already won a MC in the fighting before Dunkirk; and he possessed a profound knowledge of dock installations, for his father was Dock Master of Cardiff docks.

The story Pritchard told us was to the effect that we were being trained in the destruction of dock installations. The reason he gave, and it sounded plausible enough, was that if the Germans were to invade Britain and capture our ports, then we, the Commandos, were to be landed from the sea, behind the German invading forces, and blow up our own dock installations before they could be used by the Germans to supply their invading forces.

The port of Burntisland is small and, after a few days, we had theoretically destroyed all there was to be destroyed – ships as well! So now what? Into a train again and, many hours later, we arrived at Cardiff.

Cardiff was different. Despite wartime restrictions it had an air of friendliness and warmth about it and we enjoyed the break – so different from the cold, dark atmosphere of Burntisland (we had not been allowed even to visit Edinburgh). Barry Docks at Cardiff also posed very different problems, for Barry, with its enormous ebb and flow of tidal waters – 40 ft every 12 hours – illustrated, perhaps better than any of the other ports we had been to, how vulnerable a man-made dock can be, for, once it is destroyed, the very action of tidal waters hinders and, in a case like Cardiff, even prohibits the use of the dock until it is rebuilt. Another factor which had become increasingly apparent was the difficulty of destroying such installations by air attack. The weight of bombs then available was not powerful enough to do anything more than slight damage and, in those early wartime years, the only certain way to immobilise a dock was through the use of trained soldiers. Even towards the end of the war with the increasing might of the RAF and USAAF the Allies found difficulty in solving that same problem – how to immobilise effectively a docking system which was exposed to the open sea or tidal rivers, except possibly by using 'block ships'.

By now we almost dreamt explosives, and had become increasingly aware of the vulnerable points of pump-houses, of the machinery driving dock gates and of where and how to immobilise the giant caissons* of dry-docks effectively. There was also the ever-tempting prospect of destroying and cutting the legs off 50-ft high dockside cranes which ran on railway lines along each side of the dock to unload or load the ships berthed alongside.

But Barry Docks soon palled too and we were not sorry when, a few days later, we took the train again, this time to Southampton. There was another Engineer officer, Pritchard's assistant instructor, also from the Special Service Brigade: Captain R.K. 'Bob' Montgomery.

The character of Southampton since pre-war and early war-time days had changed. It had been one of the largest passenger liner terminals in the country; but by 1942, although the city had been badly bombed, the docks were still virtually intact, although empty and deserted, for the Luftwaffe was still too close to allow freedom of movement for our shipping. When we arrived we had the whole dock area to ourselves and, particularly, the giant King George V Dock, then the second largest in

---

* Caisson: a watertight structure placed across the entrance of a dry-dock; it is a word always used in naval language instead of 'gate'.

the world, 365.8 m long, 41.1 m wide, 14.9 m deep, with a
capacity of 39 million gallons, big enough to berth *Queen Mary*,
75,000 tons. The dock was unharmed and we practised there
day and night in and amongst its complex machinery and
enormous geographical proportions.

To destroy a dry-dock of such magnitude seemed to be an
impossibility. But we were being instructed by experts, and
practised blindfold by day so that at night we could move about
the dry-dock without fear of falling or damaging ourselves.

The rest of the team – there were ninety of us – were practising similar destruction: of winding stations which controlled
the huge caissons when the dock was full of water, over 280,000
tons of it; of the power station which drove the heavy
machinery; of the swing bridges which opened and closed to
allow movement of shipping; and of the cranes which operated
the docks. Also, we practised each other's tasks. Then, after
several days of this intensive training, we moved yet again, this
time back to Falmouth, the largest deep-water port in the West
of England, where No 5 Commando had lived for the whole of
the previous year, 1941. But we were not to see much of
Falmouth this time. We were hustled on board a ship which was
tied up alongside the docks. This ship, an ex-Cross Channel
ferry boat, *Princess Josephine Charlotte* – HMS *PJC*, as we
called her – was the sister ship of vessels on board which we had
lived in Scotland during training the previous year; and she was
to be our home from 15 to 26 March.

The ship was crowded for about 200 or more troops from No
2 Commando were already living on board having just sailed
down in her from Scotland and tied up in Falmouth Docks
waiting for us to join them, so we had to sleep on the decks and
wherever we could find room. In my case, the wardroom. This
meant I had to wait until the drinking stopped – not too difficult
an assignment – but it also meant that my sleeping-time was not
always as long as I would have liked.

It was now becoming increasingly evident that we were being
trained for something other than just the remote possibility of

countering the efforts of the Germans should they land on our coasts; and one afternoon shortly after our arrival all the army officers then on board – thirty-eight of us, all Commandos – were mustered into the wardroom and there introduced by Colonel Charles Newman, Commanding Officer of No 2 Commando, to a resplendent figure in Royal Navy uniform with three very impressive 'straight stripes' on each sleeve and with one medal on his jacket – the white ribbon of the Polar medal (with clasp). We were all young, and a Polar medal, of which there were few awarded, made a special impression on us. Also, did his medal indicate a visit to the Arctic for us – Norway again?

Our curiosity was soon allayed when the naval officer, Commander R.E.D. Ryder, stood up and told us that the target we were going to attack was a port on the coast of France.

3

The Purpose of the Raid

Throughout 1941 the Battle of the Atlantic had increased in ferocity, but in Germany's favour, with alarming losses to our merchant fleets. Our protective convoys were attacked and penetrated almost at will by German U-boats. Worse, the enemy's enormous capital ships, then hiding in the fjords of the Norwegian coast and in the Baltic, threatened to enter the Atlantic and join in the attack. And, sure enough, they did so in May 1941 when the 56,000-ton *Bismarck* and the heavy cruiser *Prinz Eugen* were discovered sailing through the Denmark Straits. Thanks to the courage of the Navy, and despite the loss of HMS *Hood*, then Britain's largest battle-cruiser, *Bismark* was finally caught, damaged and eventually sunk – on the way to her only possible haven, St Nazaire, on the French Atlantic coast.

This brought relief of a kind, but her sister ship *Tirpitz* was still lying in wait off Norway, together with other heavy vessels such as *Scharnhorst* and *Gneisenau*, to try the same tactic. At the same time our American allies had lost many of their capital ships at Pearl Harbor and elsewhere in the Pacific, while the British had lost *Prince of Wales* and *Repulse* as the Japanese had swept down the China Sea and occupied Singapore and South-East Asia.

Such was the adverse balance of sea power in 1941-2; and it was vital therefore that St Nazaire be destroyed before any further damage was done to the Allies, for if the Battle of the Atlantic was lost, then the whole war could be lost. St Nazaire at that time was the most heavily defended port outside Germany, equalled only by Brest. Her main anti-aircraft and coastal defences numbered over ninety guns of calibres ranging from 105, 88 to 40 and 20 mm. Most were multi-purpose anti-aircraft and coastal defence artillery. The dry-dock, the focal point of the port, was the largest in the world, and aircraft from Britain were not then capable of putting it out of action.

During a meeting in London when the possibility of a raid was being canvassed, Admiral Mountbatten, Director of Combined Operations, said: 'It is such an improbable scheme, they (the Germans) won't even think of it – so I can probably get you there undetected.'

Admiral of the Fleet Sir Dudley Pound, the First Sea Lord, then said: 'If it can be achieved it will be equivalent to an attack by two divisions of soldiers.'

General Montgomery, then GOC of Forces in Southern England, quick as always, said: 'No. You mean two battle-ships!'

Such was the burden of Commander Ryder's account of the strategic background situation. Now he began to describe to us the tactical role of the Commando operation. Uncovering a model of the large dock he quickly described the plan: to destroy the dry-dock and other installations there, so that if, as was feared, the German battleship *Tirpitz* ventured out into the Atlantic, she would not be able to complete the wide swing round through the Atlantic into the safety of this port, as had been the intention of *Bismarck*.

For several days after this we lived on board *Princess Josephine Charlotte* familiarising ourselves with every detail of the model of the port which had been so minutely and painstakingly made by the Photographic Reconnaissance Unit at RAF Medmenham in Berkshire.

Today that model is in the Imperial War Museum. It reflects the very high standard of Intelligence and aerial photography from which the model was constructed over forty years ago. Everything is to scale and represents an area of about a quarter by half a mile. It includes a submarine basin, submarine pens, and various dock entrances and the very large dry-dock. The Normandie dry-dock at St Nazaire, even though it was the

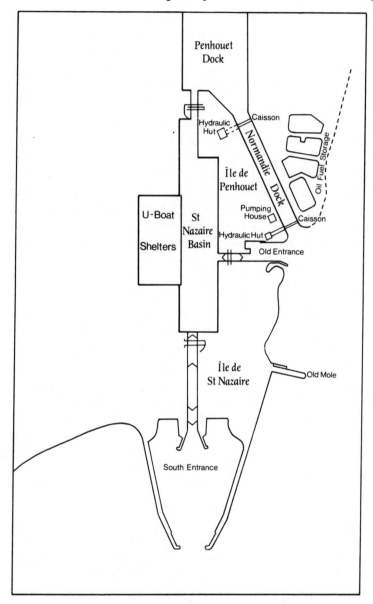

Fig. 1   St Nazaire: plan of the docks; the Normandie Dock is
1148 ft long

largest in the world, was not so long as the dock at Southampton where we had practised. It was 350 m long, 50 m wide and over 18 m deep, with a capacity of 47 million gallons. By squinting at the model from eye-level we were able to build up a picture of this port and what we would have to do when we landed there. Our recent experiences in Burntisland, Cardiff and Southampton now began to make sense, for the geography and feel of a deep-sea port was almost second nature to us.

More vessels arrived at Falmouth, including two flotillas of Motor Launches – MLs from the workhorse flotillas of coastal forces in the Royal Navy, Nos 7, 20 and 28 – and a small but lethal-looking torpedo boat, MTB 74, which was literally nothing more than two enormous torpedo tubes driven by five large engines. It had a speed reported to be in excess of 40 knots. More troops arrived and joined us.

The whole flotilla of MLs then made a practice run up the coast of Cornwall and simulated a dummy attack on Plymouth, where we were soundly defeated by the enthusiastic defence force of the Home Guard – for 'Dad's Army' was very alert that night.

Another training voyage was made by the MLs to the Scilly Isles in the most appalling weather which did no one much good – rather the contrary. Everyone was heartily seasick, and so rough was the sea that the MLs wallowed in the troughs of the enormous Atlantic waves for hour upon hour and rarely saw each other all the way to the Scilly Isles or on the return to Falmouth.

Those of us who were left behind on the *PJC* were luckier; we confined our energies to a gentle march in the lovely countryside of Cornwall, then bathing in an early spring sun. Our only fear was that we would be recognised. But we had removed our shoulder flashes and all signs of Commando identity.

In fact, security was our main preoccupation and we were not very favourably impressed when a RAF officer, Squadron Leader Evans – the famous escaper from the First World War and writer of several books on the subject – boarded the ship and gave us a talk on escaping and what to do if we should be left behind in France. The trouble was that he addressed us over the loud-hailer system of the ship. Not only could his voice be heard all over the Falmouth Docks, but, tied up alongside our ship, was a water-supply boat with the crew standing with their hands in their pockets listening to every word the Squadron Leader had to say! On the whole, however, security was good and when *PJC* moved away from the dockside and dropped anchor in the middle of Carrick Roads we felt more secure. There was the occasional visitor including friends of ours, and my own colonel from No 5 Commando, Lt-Colonel W.S.S. Sanguinetti, somehow bluffed his way on board; but, in doing so, they were again jeopardising the operation. In retrospect, it was a miracle that security was maintained in a large seaport – always the most vulnerable place to secure even to this day.

Then one morning a strange-looking vessel appeared and dropped anchor a few cables away. She had two raked funnels – a destroyer, but foreign to all the British vessels in the *Jane's Fighting Ships* of that era. She was HMS *Campbeltown*, but we did not then realise her significance to us.

HMS *Campbeltown* was once an American destroyer, the USS *Buchanan*, and although built for active service in the First World War she was named and commissioned too late for hostilities – on 2 January 1919.

USS *Buchanan* first served out of Guantanamo in Cuba. In 1922, she was placed in 'care and maintenance' at San Diego. After successive tours of active duty, and in reserve, by the time that Pearl Harbor was bombed in 1941, the *Buchanan*, luckily, was serving off the Atlantic coast.

Then fate played a mysterious hand in the affairs of *Buchanan*. She was suddenly and dramatically transferred to the 'flag' of the Royal Navy, when President Roosevelt traded fifty of America's 'four-stacker' First World War destroyers for leases of British bases in the West Indies and Newfoundland.

By 1942 *Campbeltown* was a well-tried and 'blooded'

warship. During this period she was commanded by a Lt T.W.T. Beloe, RN, and later by a distinguished officer, Lt-Cdr The Lord Teynham, RN.

Campbeltown was then converted for the raid on St Nazaire to look like a German Möwe class Torpedo Boat Destroyer. To this end two of her four 'stacks' or funnels were removed, and the tops of the remaining two were cut on a slant to give her a distinctly 'foreign', almost rakish, appearance. She was completely rearmed with eight Oerlikon guns.

Campbeltown was quite fast. She was 1154 tons in weight, 314 feet long and she was lightened so that at speed she could just clear the main sandbanks which guarded the entrance to the River Loire from the sea, by a foot or so.

Campbeltown was expendable and those of us on board knew that. We also realised that when the German defences fired on us, with some 100 guns of all calibres, we would be in grave danger of being damaged to the point of losing mobility, and in danger of sinking before we reached our objective.

Everything was now coming together, so we were not surprised when once again we were called to a meeting below decks in *PJC* with our NCOs and soldiers and told by Colonel Newman we were ready to go.

He went on to explain that the raid had a high element of risk and that we could not expect any guarantee of a safe return. If there were those who were married, or who had reservations about going on the raid, now was the time to say so, with no reason to be ashamed or fear of being criticised. Various people have described this episode and tried to explain our reaction and expressions at such a suggestion. All I can remember is one of silence at being told by the colonel what was at stake – a relaxed silence, one of acceptance despite the risks. There were no rude noises, as some people have indicated. We were, after all, trained soldiers and not in the habit of expressing ourselves to our Commanding Officer in words or sounds of disrespect.

Even so, we understood well what he was trying to convey to us. We were expendable.

4

We Dress for Battle

On the morning of 26 March 1942, a Thursday, we were told to get dressed in full battle order and prepare for embarkation. At midday we were ferried in small groups from *PJC*, our carrier ship, to the sixteen MLs, an MTB, and MGB and the foreign-looking destroyer (nineteen vessels in all).

By early afternoon the MGB and the MLs had slipped away to the open sea to be followed by *Campbeltown* towing MTB 74 to conserve her fuel. Once out to sea we were escorted by a lone fighter aircraft, a Hurricane, from St Eval airfield in the north of Cornwall – and, later, by an occasional twin-engined Beaufighter.

The small vessels were formed into two columns to simulate an anti-submarine sweep. We on board *Campbeltown*, towing the MTB, were in the van, sailing aft of MGB 314, being towed by HMS *Atherstone* (commanded by Robin Jenks, Lt-Cdr, RN), a Hunt class destroyer in which Lt-Cdr Ryder and Lt-Colonel Newman were to establish their floating Headquarters, and we were followed by the two columns of MLs, eight in each column. We made about 14 knots, mostly to conserve fuel and also to facilitate towing MTB 74. Incidentally, MTB 74's highly tuned engines had been giving trouble before our departure and it was not too certain if they would work properly when she was cast off under her own power.

Shortly after slipping our moorings in the Carrick Roads we were joined by another Hunt class destroyer, *Tynedale*. Later two other Hunt class destroyers, *Brocklesby* and *Cleveland*, were sent to join us, but it was too late for them to have any effect other than to pick up any wounded adrift in the sea.

Apart from the crews of the two covering destroyers (some

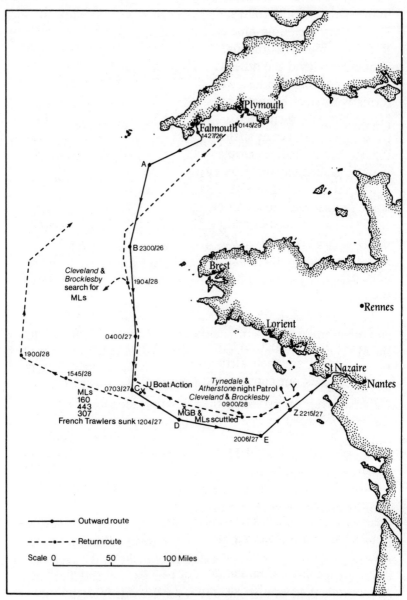

Fig. 2   Plan showing outward and return routes

300 all ranks), and escorting aircraft, the actual raiding force numbered 611 sailors and soldiers; approximately half of them Royal Navy including nine junior Dominion officers from the RNVR – four Australians, three Canadians and two New Zealanders – and the other half Army Commandos.

We, the Commandos, were wearing our battle-dress uniforms with steel helmets; the now famous green Commando berets had not then been issued. We wore heavy navy-blue jerseys and duffel coats so that when we were on deck we hoped that to any inquisitive aeroplane we would look like sailors. We in the Commandos were from many Regiments and Corps in the British Army including Guardsmen, a preponderance of Highland troops and men from county Regiments especially Lancastrians, Geordies and a handful of Irishmen. Similarly, we had a high proportion of officers – thirty-eight – for such a small force, including a significant sprinkling from Territorial units of the 60th, the King's Royal Rifle Corps, known today as the Green Jackets.

The coast of France was only a few miles away on our port side and our overriding fear was of discovery by German reconnaissance planes which, at that time, were sweeping far out over the Atlantic from their airfields in France to help their submarines attack our convoys. But luck was on our side and we saw nothing that day.

One further device was used to help obscure our identity: we flew the Nazi flag from the masthead of *Campbeltown*. It was an eerie feeling to look up at our masthead and see that sinister and frightening enemy flag fluttering in the light sea breeze, which ruffled its deadly design – a black swastika on a red background. Accepted from time immemorial as a *ruse de guerre*, would the Germans think the same if they saw us and subsequently realised our true colours? That flag was to have a vital role in the raid.

As night fell we Commandos took turns helping the sailors keep watch. The weather was completely calm; I dread to think what would have been the result if it had deteriorated with heavy seas causing seasickness and exhaustion before we ever reached our target area. As we kept watch with our naval hosts, we were introduced to the questionable comforts of 'purser's cocoa' – cocoa chipped from a solid block into a mug and diluted with scalding hot water and generous lashings of condensed milk and sugar, producing a mixture so thick that you 'could stand your spoon up in it'. But it was hot and a great luxury in the cold night air. We also had drinks served on the bridge, probably one of the few times in history that this has happened on a warship going into action.

The next morning found us making 8 knots 150 miles out into the Atlantic, bearing south by west in a wide sweep round Finistère and down into the Bay of Biscay. Our speed had been cut back to minimise our wash in case we were spotted by German air patrols. By this time our escorting aircraft had long since left us and we were on our own.

There was an alarm when we saw and attacked a German submarine. The submarine did report seeing our escorting destroyers but, in its efforts to crash-dive and escape our attacks, the submarine had failed to see *us* or the MLs as these were too low in the water. In any event, the Germans took no action on receiving the report – surprising but miraculous again.

Another unwelcome distraction then appeared in the shape of several French inshore fishing vessels, the equivalent of today's Seine netters. For some reason which was never explained to us, two of these vessels were boarded by the Navy, the French crews taken on board the escorting Hunt class destroyers and the two fishing vessels sunk by gunfire. The strange thing about this limited action was that the other fishing vessels were left unharmed and we sailed on leaving them behind us as we were reassured that they had no contact with the enemy, but we could not help but wonder if they would give the alarm to the Germans. During the long hours that followed we rested and even lay out on deck in the warm sun of that beautiful March weather. But, to maintain concentration, it was then decided to check our equipment once again, explosives and armaments. We unpacked our rucksacks and checked each small packet of explosive – some 60 lb each of packages and fuses per officer and man broken down into small parcels wrapped in brown water-proof paper varying from ½ lb to 2 lb in weight – in other words the explosives were already prepared ready to be placed in their allocated positions for destruction. We then repacked them carefully in the order in which they were to be used. The explosive used was the latest and more stable – unlike gun-cotton. It was called 'plastic' for its malleable characteristics.

It is difficult to describe what we felt at that time. We were curiously relaxed, light-hearted even, glad to get away from the hustle of preparation and planning and knowing that we were involved in a total commitment of our own making and with no going back. Further than that we did not dare conjecture and during that voyage in the calm of early spring weather, I, for one, did a lot of quiet praying.

We were not entirely cut off from our base in England, for although we could make no signals back to Falmouth or to the Admiralty, we could receive radio messages and had the satis-faction of being told that the enemy had no suspicion of our presence or our intentions although more patrol vessels had arrived at St Nazaire and were anchored neatly alongside each other in the inland dock. Other than this unexpected and unwelcome addition to the German presence there was no other extraordinary activity worthy of note.

As the day wore on we began to realise that our ship, *Camp-beltown*, was on a one-way ticket and that everything on board her was doomed to destruction. Precisely how we were not sure, but clearly she was to be used as some kind of block ship. As of one accord, the sailors and soldiers embarked on a great opening of cupboards and unearthed all kinds of items of old uniform and equipment. The result was a mad fancy-dress party led by one of my closest friends in No 5 Commando, Robert Burten-shaw – a giant of a man. He was in the Cheshire Regiment; educated at Sedbergh; an extremely good second row forward; a man who, unbelievably, wore a monocle, much to the delight of the Yorkshire and Lancastrian soldiers in his troop, who nick-named him 'Bertie Bagwash'. Sadly, he was to meet his death the next morning, but his bravery was recognised by a post-humous Mention in Dispatches, the only recognition, other than a VC, which was then awarded to the dead. Wearing the naval cap of our Captain, Lt-Commander S.H. Beattie, he took over command of the ship and parodied the Senior Service to the delight of everyone on board.

We had no Press photographers with us, but two war corres-pondents, Gordon Holman of the London *Evening Standard*, and E.J. Gilling of the Exchange Telegraph.

I had a small Kodak camera with me, which perhaps broke the rules, but if I had succeeded in keeping or hiding that film it would have been a wonderful record of that strange day – the last day on earth for so many of those who took part in the raid.

We slept most of that afternoon – for we would have no sleep that night. The evening was quiet and uneventful and dusk turned to night. But it was not a dark night and the sea was so calm it reminded me of the crossing from Dunkirk, the night I had escaped from France two years before.

We sailed steadily on with a feeling of relief that the night was once again masking our presence. By this time we were about a hundred miles off the coast of France and we dozed fitfully in our bunks until it was time for an early supper. Together with our naval hosts (incidentally, the crew of *Campbeltown* had been reduced to the very minimum of 6 officers and 69 other ranks compared with its normal complement of 146 or more) we met in the wardroom and finished off the excellent La Ina sherry. Wine was non-existent in those days and we purposely did not drink anything stronger.

Strangely, those of us who were there that night seem to have little or no memory of what we had to eat on board *Campbel-town*. By general consensus we think it was a hot stew and we all agree that although it was the last meal to be served on *Campbeltown* it was very tasty and well cooked.

We started to get ready for the raid. We still had some two hours' sailing and it was planned that we would rendezvous 40 miles from St Nazaire with the submarine HMS *Sturgeon*, commanded by Lt-Commander M.R.G. Wingfield, RN. Commander Wingfield had recently been awarded the DSO for sinking a ship in the Trondheim Fjord despite the minefields he had had to dive under to achieve his objective. Before that, he had been operating in the waters of north Russia, based at Polyarnoe on the Kola Inlet, and under the Command of the C-in-C Soviet Northern Fleet, Admiral Golikov.

Commander Wingfield takes up the story:

In early March, after many more patrols and a few successes off the Norwegian coast, we were ordered to Plymouth where I was told of the part I was to play in the raid on St Nazaire. I remember well the briefing meeting where nearly everyone had some comment to make or question to ask – except, that is, one naval officer who was totally silent. I asked him what role he had in the operation to which he replied, 'I am the naval commander.' Ryder was never very chatty.

We sailed on board *Sturgeon* from Plymouth on 25 March and, diving by day, proceeded to a position outside St Nazaire where we were to act as a beacon to the raiding force. I fixed my position with some accuracy by taking periscope bearings all during the afternoon of 27 March. We must have been fairly close to shore as I remember fixing our position many times during that day (27 March) by periscope bearings on conspicuous shore features. The sea was glassy calm and there were many fishing vessels in the area. When it was dark, I surfaced and charged batteries. Some time around midnight (22.00 was the reported time) I started flashing the letter 'M' (dash-dash) on a shaded lamp showing towards the direction of approach of the raiding force, that is from the sou'-sou'-west. I remember being somewhat apprehensive that the fishing vessels would raise the alarm if they saw us but they took no notice although some of them were fairly close.

Sturgeon, an 'S' class submarine, had a crew of between 50 and 60 officers and men and was in fact heavier than *Campbeltown* with a tonnage of about one thousand three hundred. Apart from *Sturgeon* most of the 'S' class were sunk during the war. Like all submarines they operated under the direct command of the Admiral (Submarines) but in this particular case the *Sturgeon* was lent to Admiral Sir Charles Forbes, the C-in-C Plymouth, for the raid.

At about 23.30 hours some ships came into view (23.14 hours, in fact). I recall seeing *Campbeltown*, whose captain gave me a wave, and I certainly saw *Atherstone* because her captain used his loud-hailer to greet me with a loud 'Hullo, Mervyn.' He was Robin Jenks, son of a former Lord Mayor of London and a regular naval officer. His normal stentorian tones amplified to excess – 'Are you in the right place?' 'Yes,' I replied, 'within a hundred yards, but don't make so much noise!' Every fisherman within a couple of miles must have heard him and we had reports that the Germans had armed some of these fishing vessels as part of the harbour defences. However, none of them took the slightest notice of us and the long line of small ships continued shorewards into the early morning mist. The sea was still flat calm and it seemed to us that complete surprise was achieved.

When the last of the raiding force had disappeared towards the coast Commander Wingfield said: 'My job was complete and I proceeded in accordance with previous orders to patrol an area off Brest to the north. *Sturgeon* took no part in the withdrawal from the raid, but we heard plenty of loud explosions.'

Strangely enough, Wingfield reports that, apart from my letters to him – he was then, when I wrote to him, a retired Captain living in Surrey – he was pleased to be asked about his participation in the raid as no one else has ever taken much interest in his activities on that day. On reflection is it strange that the part played by *Sturgeon* has only ever been mentioned a few times for, although the precise navigation of Commander Ryder and his navigating officer Lieutenant A.R. Green was of pinpoint accuracy, the fact remains that had the weather worsened to gale force, Commander Wingfield's* positioning of his submarine as a beacon would have been invaluable. Green, himself, who, as navigating officer to Commander Ryder, was in charge of navigation for the whole force, has told me that Commander Wingfield's positioning of *Sturgeon* was accurate to within a cable's-length of our course and a very reassuring check for his own navigation. What Commander Wingfield does not mention is that – possibly unconsciously – he acted as a 'marker' to ML 446 which had broken down and fallen behind the main force. Under power once again, however, they nearly collided with *Sturgeon* as she dived away. The ML sailed on only to be scuttled with heavy casualties during the attack.

We had over thirty miles to go and as we sped nearer the coast we could see the glow of searchlights in the sky and, shortly afterwards, the sound of aircraft indicated that other friends, the RAF, had arrived to distract the enemy from seeing us. I remember thinking that the scene was no different from other air raids we had been witness to since 1940. But this time there *was* a difference: we wanted this air raid and we wanted it to continue until we arrived right in the middle of it.

We began to take up our prearranged positions for disembarkation. Those of us who were to land first were to lie on deck and those who were to land after us went down below decks in strict order of disembarkation.

The only people who were allowed to stand on deck during the run-in were the gun crews on the 'bandstands' which housed the eight Oerlikon quick-fire guns and the 12-pounder gun on the forward deck. The Oerlikon guns – four on each side of the ship – gave an overall field of fire protecting the ship from stem to stern.

To give the Commandos protection from enemy fire the Navy had fitted four rows of metal screens riveted to the deck running

---

* Wingfield went on to command other submarines and later that year, 1942, his submarine took part in the North African landings which preceded the defeat of the Germans in North Africa.

aft from the main bridge structure right back to the stern of the ship. They were 1 ft 6 in. high, just high enough to protect us from small-arms fire and the light cannon fire we expected. But they were of little protection against direct hits from the heavy naval guns we knew to be part of the German defences.

We were to lie on the deck on our backs, feet first, so as to cushion the shock of impact when *Campbeltown* crashed, as planned, into the dry-dock gates.

Having organised my own team into their proper places and helped them place their heavy rucksacks full of explosives behind and under their heads for extra protection from the impending impact, I slipped below decks to wish good luck to my friends, Robert Burtenshaw and Christopher Smalley and the men in their teams, all from my own Commando No 5.

My own team was made up of sergeants from No 1 Commando, and there was a fair degree of interchange between the officers and men from Nos 1, 2, 3, 4, 5, 9 and 12 Commandos who provided the demolition element of the raiding force.

'Bertie', the extrovert, was cheerful, whilst Smalley was quiet. I remember helping them tear down the blackout curtains screening their cabin doors so as to facilitate their quick exit and reduce the risk of fire. I also said a few special words to my own troop sergeants, Frank Carr, and McKerr, both regular soldiers – Sappers – tough and the backbone of the demolition team commanded by Burtenshaw.

This done I went back up on deck and lay down ahead of my own team and just behind a young, fair-haired sergeant called Davies from No 3 Commando. The sound of aircraft grew louder and apart from the smell of the sea there was a new, exciting smell – a whiff of the country, France, a smell distinctive as garlic and Gauloise cigarettes. We were very close!

Although I had a wrist-watch I did not think of checking the time; I was content to leave everything to the Navy – for they were in charge.

The noise of aircraft continued, but then seemed to get less. Shortly afterwards the noise of planes died away altogether and, one by one, the searchlights ahead of us were dimmed, leaving the coastline in darkness again.

The last few miles of our approach to St Nazaire are described with great accuracy by Commander Ryder in his account and amplified by Brigadier Lucas Phillips in *The Greatest Raid of All*. Briefly, we sailed on, still undetected and still flying the Nazi flag, and increasing speed to some 15 knots as we approached the sandbanks which we had to cross using the deeper water of the spring tides, avoiding the main swept channel and German guardships. We could not increase speed too much, however, because the Navy had discovered that the stern of *Campbeltown* dug down into the water at speed, thereby defeating the object of our, so far, secret voyage. We had to keep speed down so that the buoyancy of our ship would enable her to ride over the sandbanks into clearer water the other side. We, the passengers on *Campbeltown*, had been told what the plan of approach was to be, but we were not to appreciate fully the delicacy of the clearance with which the Navy had calculated our run-in for, suddenly at 00.45 hrs, there was a fearful juddering and our whole ship shook from stem to stern as we scraped across some sandbanks. Then, a few seconds later at 00.55 hrs, we slowed again as our propeller screws somehow drove us across yet another sandbar. We all held our breath and suddenly we were in clear water again. We had lightened the ship during our run-in by throwing overboard every item of unnecessary equipment but, as the ship was already stripped of most unwanted gear, there was little we could do. As Donald Roy, who was to lead the soldiers' assault from *Campbeltown*, said, 'We felt a churning and shuddering through the mud and we had some bad moments particularly the second time we stuck.' Suffice to say that if we had not cleared those sandbanks we would have been 'stopped' to provide a sitting target for every German gun in the area and the raid would have been a complete failure.

The smaller and lighter vessels had no problem other than keeping station, particularly MTB 74 which was now under her own power and proceeding in a series of stops and starts to contain her great acceleration.

To give an idea of the 'stopping factor' the mud had on our movement, Commander Beattie said that as he looked over the side of the ship to see if we were still moving he noted that *Campbeltown*'s speed was checked to about 5 knots – 5 knots between maintaining way and 'stop' – and disaster. To me those few moments of shuddering and shaking aboard *Campbeltown* were the most dramatic of our whole approach until our actual arrival.

As Brigadier Lucas Phillips recorded after the war, the professional Loire pilots declared that Green's feat of navigation (up the Loire and over the sandbanks) that night was 'without parallel in the history of the port'.

There was still no sign from the enemy. Some say there was a light rain, but I don't remember any. On the contrary, I recollect that it was a calm night with light cloud a few thousand feet high, but sufficiently thick to mask the targets from the air.

At that time Churchill had ordered that no attack was to be made on French military targets unless they could be closely identified. St Nazaire was undoubtedly a No 1 military target with its U-boat pens and the dry-dock facilities so valuable to the Germans. When, therefore, the light cloud obscured the port and the old town of St Nazaire (now no longer in existence), the RAF bombers were called off, leaving us to go on alone and face the consequences. Years later, at the end of the war, our colonel, Charles Newman, having just returned from a prison camp and been awarded the Victoria Cross, was invited to dine at Chartwell by Churchill. After dinner the Prime Minister said, 'Newman, I want you to come with me,' and he led him into the rose garden, undid his flies and relieved himself, saying, 'I'm sorry about St Nazaire, and leaving you alone with no air support; six months later I wouldn't have bothered.'

Newman murmured some reassuring words. But at the same time he wondered how many other men had received an apology from Churchill at that time – or ever!

When we had cleared the sandbanks, we increased speed. Closer and closer we sailed – we had under two miles to go, but suddenly it was evident we had been seen. The Germans were uncertain, however, and while they were arguing, flashing signals to each other – from ship to shore and back to the guard ships – we were closing at 18½ knots – in landlubber's jargon, nearly 20 mph.

Suddenly we were conscious of increasing German activity and light firing just ahead of us. Then a searchlight found us, but immediately dimmed again as our naval signalman, Leading Signalman Pike, on board the command vessel MGB 314, flashed reassuring messages in German to our challengers. Every second counted and, as the Germans uncertainly wondered what to do, we sped on. We had not far to go – but three minutes from zero hour, 01.30,* the Germans again opened fire and the whole of *Campbeltown* was bathed in light.

Realising we had been discovered, the German flag was run down and slowly, almost reluctantly, a somewhat bedraggled and not very clean White Ensign broke at the masthead – and all down the columns of motor launches other White Ensigns broke.

The blaze of light from the searchlights increased and it seemed as if we could only last for a few seconds more before either losing control and foundering, or at worst exploding into smithereens. At least that is what I thought. Such was the intensity of fire directed at us that Tom Boyd, one of the most distinctive participants of the raid who miraculously survived the river battle commanding ML 160, declared, 'The weight of fire caught one's breath.' Colonel Newman, looking back at us from his command post on MGB 34, said of *Campbeltown*, 'Her sides seemed to be alive with bursting shells.'

Lying on the deck of *Campbeltown* we were perhaps not so conscious of the fire being directed at us, except that every now

* We actually arrived at 01.34 hrs, four minutes late.

and then there would be an explosion, a clanging of metal and of steel on steel and a struggling movement among the Commandos lying there indicating that someone had been wounded. As we looked up at the two Oerlikon bandstands just forward of where we were lying, we saw them firing furiously in reply to the German guns. Suddenly the gunlayer manning his Oerlikon on the starboard side threw up his arms and collapsed. As he fell, his gun swung aimlessly up and into the sky, counter-balancing the weight of his dead or dying body in his gunlayer's sling; but the other Oerlikons proceeded to pump a non-stop fire of shells in retaliation and as I peeked over the top of our steel protecting barriers I was conscious of ships burning alongside us and to our stern. It was a silly and extremely dangerous action and I shouted sharply to some of the soldiers near me: 'Get your bloody heads down!'

Then there was another explosion and a large report rather like the noise of someone banging a steel door with a sledge-hammer. It was caused by a shell which burst alongside me and as I lay there dazed and deafened I wondered what had happened to me. Then suddenly I realised that Sergeant Davies of No 3 Commando lying just ahead of me had been hit, for his immediate reaction was to try and struggle to his feet, but I kept him still by wrapping my legs round his shoulders. It was then that I realised that my left leg was wet and sticky and my right arm was spurting blood down into my hand. I, too, had been hit, but by some twist of fate there was no pain – just discomfort. As I passed my tongue over my lips I tasted small particles of dust and a powder-like substance which had a sweet-sickly flavour of almonds – nitroglycerine – so close had we been to the epicentre of the shell's explosion. I then realised that my hands, which had been shading my tin hat over my eyes, were also covered in blood, but again there was no pain, only a new-found stiffness in my fingers and numerous pinpricks in my face. I didn't realise it then but I was literally peppered with minute pieces of shell all down the front and left side of my body from my face to my legs, but when I wiped the blood off my face there was little or nothing to show what had happened. I began to feel myself all over looking for further damage, but fortunately I still seemed to be intact and mobile.

Others had been wounded, but there was nothing we could do but lie 'doggo' and hope to survive the non-stop barrage of fire which was by this time coming at us at point-blank range.

There were fires blazing on the surface of the river astern of us where more of our MLs were fighting their desperate battle for survival against the overwhelming fire-power of the German guns – nearly one hundred of them.

Meanwhile, high up on the open bridge of *Campbeltown*, Commander 'Sam' Beattie, with his small party, was steering the ship ever nearer to our destination. When the German fire grew in intensity, Beattie ordered everyone down from the fighting top into the armoured wheelhouse where at least there was some protection. Even so, the coxswain, Chief Petty Officer Wellsted, immediately fell dead. His place at the wheel was taken by the Quartermaster, but he was also killed. Then Montgomery took over the wheel momentarily, until Beattie's explosives officer, Lieutenant Nigel Tibbets, calmly took his place. As Montgomery said: 'My thoughts as I grabbed the wheel were, "Port left as it is shorter and Red for the wine." '

He went on: 'There was so much light from the shells and their tracers, and the searchlights, that we really couldn't see. It was "Sam" Beattie's decision, I suppose, that really "made" the raid. For had he not ordered a change in our course we would have hit the Old Mole sticking, as it was, right out into the river in front of us. The feeling of relief when Tibbets took over was over-whelming – it had only been a few seconds but it felt like an age.' Meanwhile 'Sam' Beattie quietly gave his orders: 'Hard a-starboard'; Tibbets acknowledged 'Hard a-starboard, sir – steer 055 degrees' and answering his command the destroyer swung to starboard – 'port 25 – steer 345 degrees'. Then Beattie made a correction – how he could see, let alone keep calm control of a ship of over 1000 tons moving at 20 knots, can only be understood by professional seamen. He then ordered 'Steer 350 degrees' and Tibbets swung the ship back to starboard – his right – with only 700 yds to go to the dock gates.

Meanwhile every German gun that could bear on us was firing non-stop. We were repeatedly hit and we were suffering heavy casualties in both dead and wounded – soldiers and sailors alike. The forward deck was covered with wounded. The ship was on fire, and those of us midships and in the stern were mostly wounded. If it had not been for the small steel screens we would have suffered even more seriously. There was nothing we could do except lie there and await our arrival.

Although I did not realise it at the time we were being given great assistance and covering fire from Boyd and his ML 160, Irwin and his ML 270, and by our command vessel MGB 314. Almost like mother hens they were helping us home, and they gave as good as they got.

Professor R.V. Jones in his book *Most Secret War* tells how among those killed at St Nazaire was his cousin Lieutenant E.A. Beart, RNVR, commanding ML 267, who, like those in the trenches of the First World War, took a rugby ball with him with which to play on the quay while we Commandos carried out our demolition tasks. Alas, it was not to be. Beart was but one of the many who died fighting their MLs in the desperate naval battle.

Although all this action took only two or three minutes it seemed much longer; then suddenly there was a big puff of black smoke from the funnels of *Campbeltown* and with a great lurch to starboard the ship accelerated and then, following a great lunging movement as her bows cut the anti-torpedo wires and nets, she was brought suddenly judderingly to a stop, her bows jammed into and over the dock gates.

As Bob Ryder wrote, after the war: 'I can think of no other case where so much has depended on the unfaltering seamanship in action of one man. This dazzling exploit by Sam Beattie shines as the hallmark and principal achievement of the expedition.'

5

Four Minutes Late

To bring to a dead stop a ship of over 1000 tons in a matter of seconds which only a few moments before was slicing through the water at 20 knots was shattering; and it was not until a few seconds had passed – it may have been longer – that we realised we now had to face the problems which lay ahead of us. Beattie had delivered us on time, only four minutes late as we discovered later in the raid, and the rest was up to us. I somehow forced myself to stand up and get my rucksack on to my shoulders. Others near me were likewise struggling to their feet, but some there were who lay still or struggled to rise only to fall back. Firing was still going on all round us and one of my first reactions was to note the almost toy-like chatter of our Commandos' tommy-guns and stripped Lewis guns as they landed and joined in the firing. Meanwhile the heavy German counter-barrage continued.

Many years later I came to realise that if the Germans had not been so preoccupied with firing at the MTBs and the MLs they could not help but have seen us moving about on the decks of *Campbeltown*, but even if they did see us they did not seem to realise that the role of *Campbeltown* was still not finished. Had they done so, one burst of fire from a 20-mm cannon would have killed all of us, and what is more could have ignited the hundreds of pounds of explosives we were carrying between us. But we were left alone and slowly and methodically we mobilised our soldiers, and started to evacuate the ship.

By the time I led my small team forward, others had already preceded us, including the assault parties who were to clear the way for us in the event that we were opposed. We clambered forward along the sloping and slippery deck and made our way round the main bridge structure to cross the forward deck, but as we did so we encountered more dead and wounded sailors and Commandos lying where they had been caught in the murderous German fire, particularly round the 12-pounder gun which had been destroyed by a direct hit. I remember stopping and speaking to a friend among the wounded, John Proctor, a Cameron Highlander, who was lying there minus most of one of his legs. He asked us to help him, but there was nothing that we could do and we had to press on. He was later evacuated and returned safely to England.

As I turned away and made to pass the damaged gun I fell into a large shell-hole in the deck and was saved from falling further only by the bulk of my rucksack. My soldiers hauled me up out of the shell-hole and on to my feet away from the fire that was then raging below decks.

When *Campbeltown* came to a stop her bows had risen up out of the water and on to the top of the dry-dock gate. Her bows were in fact buckled back 36 ft as a result of which the whole ship was pointing up out of the water at an angle of about 20 degrees with her stern riding just above the surface – then at high water.

When we got to the ship's bows we found that there was only one scaling ladder left by the assault parties. This hung over the port side and down on to the road running across the top of the dock gates, some 30 ft wide.

The ladder was vertical and there was no question of climbing down it, so somehow we fell down it and onto the road surface – a drop of 18 ft or more. How we managed to get down the ladder I will never know. I think in some cases we must have thrown each other down from the ship's bows.

Still no one seemed to notice our presence; although German guns were firing directly over our heads the Germans amazingly did not see us. Picking ourselves up, we ran as fast as we could to the unmistakable two-storey-high pump-house which was over 75 ft wide and 150 ft long – almost identical in shape and size to the pump-house on which we had practised in Southampton.

At this point I was joined by our assault party led by the bespectacled and square little figure of Lieutenant Hopwood, Essex Regiment and No 2 Commando, whose responsibility was to make sure that I got into the pump-house without interference from the Germans. When we arrived at the door of the pump-house, however, we found it to be locked. This momentarily confused me, for of all the eventualities we had thought of, and prepared for, we had never foreseen that the pump-house doors would be locked. They were 20 ft high and built of steel and presumably were closed by the port authorities to prevent sabotage or burglary – unlike Southampton where the doors of all buildings were left open in case of air raids and fire. As I stood there wondering what to do Montgomery arrived. He took a small magnetic charge from his pocket and slapped it on the lock of the door and told me to ignite it, but my hands were trembling and very sticky with the congealing blood from the wounds in my right arm and I asked him to do it for me in case the soldiers would think I was frightened, which I was.

Montgomery lit his match and, hardly moving, we waited for the charge to burst. It did so with a small explosion and the great doors swung open. Montgomery raced away to see how the others were faring. Escorted by Lieutenant Hopwood, commander of my assault team, we entered the vast, hollow-sounding chamber of the pumping-station. Again everything was roughly the same as at Southampton and we quickly made our way across the vast floor of the station to the iron stairs which led down to the pumps 40 ft below us. When I was wounded on the deck of *Campbeltown* one of my party, Sergeant Chamberlain, was also hit and when I asked him what had happened he said that he could not walk very well as he had been wounded. When we moved, therefore, Sergeants Butler and King hauled him to his feet and, putting their arms round his shoulders, they pulled him along the deck behind them. Sergeant Dockerill, the other member of my team, meanwhile carried Chamberlain's heavy, 60 lb rucksack in addition to his own load.

When we got to the top of the stairs in the pump-house I
decided that Chamberlain should stay behind and guard us
from any trouble from the Germans and that I would take over
his demolition work and pick him up again when our job was
finished. I gave him one of my two Colt automatics as added
fire-power.

And so we slowly started to descend the metal staircase into
the blackness of the pumping-chamber, but it was different
from Southampton. Instead of the stairs leading on down, the
whole descent was punctuated with galleries which broke off
into several directions with no indication as to which one led on
down to the main staircase. We had small torch-lights attached
to our webbing belts, but their area of light was limited to a yard
or so. Slowly we made our way down through the maze of
galleries, stopping every now and then to check that we were on
the main staircase and not turning off into a blind gallery to
plunge to our deaths below.

Again luck seemed to be guiding us and apart from a few
moments of uncertainty and minor hesitations and diversions
we arrived safely on the floor of the pump-house. It was enormous, and lying there – as at Southampton – was an identical set
of four impeller pumps with a few ancillary smaller pumps to
our left – the whole of which were connected by drive shafts
from the centre of the pumps up into the night above us,
connecting the pumps to the large electric motors 15 ft or more
high which we had passed on our way across the ground floor
now above us.

Despite the absence of Chamberlain we quickly went to
work. Each of us, by a prearranged plan, attacked one pump – I
took Chamberlain's Pump No 1 – and we carefully laid about 40
lb of explosives on each of the castings and moulds of these
enormous impellers. We worked quickly and silently – just able
to see each other by the combined lights of our torches. Twenty
or so minutes later we connected all the charges to a long
ring-main of cordtex fuse and finally to a duplicate set of per-
cussion igniters which I had to fire. We had also, incidentally,

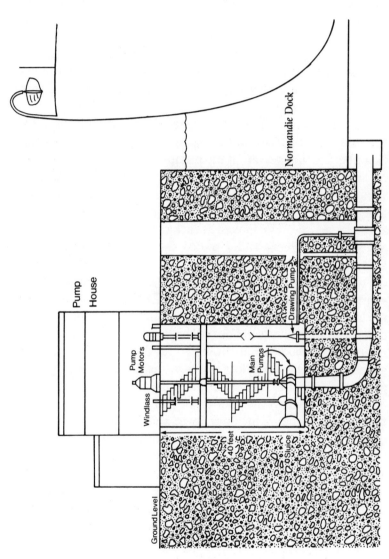

Fig. 3   Sectional view of the pumping system of the dry-dock

laid charges from my spare set of explosives on to the ancillary pumps. While we had been working there was suddenly the tremendous crash of an explosion from above. I shouted up to Chamberlain, 'What was that?' and he quickly replied, 'It's Captain Donald, sir, blowing up the guns on the roof.' It was Donald Roy, another Cameron Highlander, who with his assault force had earlier led the disembarkation of our soldiers from *Campbeltown.*

Picking up our rucksacks with a few blocks of explosives still to spare I sent Butler and King to climb the stairs, pick up Chamberlain and get out of the pump-house as fast as possible. Meanwhile Dockerill and I waited quietly until we heard them shout clearance; then, giving Dockerill one igniter, I took the other and said, 'I'll count three, then we'll pull the igniter pins at the same time.' We looked at each other as I slowly counted, one – two – three – and I pulled the pin of my igniter and Dockerill did the same. I have often wondered whether I was the one to ignite my detonator first, but I shall never know. Not stopping for another second I ordered Dockerill to go ahead of me and, clinging to his waist belt, we climbed up the stairs as quickly as we could to get out of the building. The fuse of each igniter was of 90-seconds duration and there was little time to spare in the event we lost our way in the confusion of the galleries. We got to the top of the stairs, however, without any delay and ran across the floor to the main entrance and out into the cool air of the night. So relieved was I at what we had just done and of having cleared the pump-house, I was happy just to stand there and gasp for air. Suddenly Montgomery appeared again and shouted at us to move away as fast as possible. It was lucky he did so for a few seconds later there was a deafening explosion and the large blocks of concrete protecting the building from air-raid damage flew up into the air and crashed down on the quayside where we had just been standing.

There is a well-known adage 'familiarity breeds contempt' for those who handle explosives, and several people have met their death for not observing proper safety margins. In this particular case there was so much noise and smoke and glare from the several searchlights that the sheer relief of getting out of the dark pumping-chamber 40 ft below made the danger of proximity of explosives and fire rather relative – academic even. It was just as well Montgomery was there to oversee our movements. For as he said, 'Stuart Chant and his party came out of the pumping-station and lay down on the road outside under the protective anti-blast wall. Fortunately I happened to pass by (having failed to blow up the ships in the dry-dock because of heavy fire from the enemy) and told Chant and his party to move farther away, which they somewhat reluctantly did – out of range of the heavy blocks of stone which came crashing down where they had been lying.'

Again the force of the explosion which erupted up and out of the ground from the pumping-chamber was far greater than we had expected; this was due to the 'tamping' effect the confines of the pumping-chamber had on our combined explosions and gave an added satisfaction to our success. But nothing else seemed to matter at that moment other than that we were all comparatively safe and out of sight of the German guns firing over our heads. For one fleeting second we were unmindful of the fighting and chaos of fire and smoke surrounding us.

But our job was not yet finished. We had destroyed the pumps, but we had been ordered to re-enter the pump-house and destroy the electric motors on the ground floor, four massive installations which drove the pumps, and the ancillary and smaller electrical equipment down below.

So, after a slight hesitation, I led my team back into the building to complete our task. To the surprise of Bob and myself and our almost overwhelming relief, the big electric motors – some 15 ft high – were lying at crazy angles and the floor in the centre of the chamber had partially collapsed. I had no intention of risking the safety of my sergeants any further, and apart from letting King and Dockerill smash a few oilpipes on the transformers, and dials of the electrical switchboards, there seemed little point in pressing the attack any more and, rightly or wrongly, I ordered Dockerill, Butler and King to throw their incendiary bombs into the mess and smoke, and we quickly left the building.

Again, the mere thought of falling down into that pumping-chamber, with the distinct possibility that the force of the explosion had destroyed the stairways and galleries, was something I dared not consider, having already had the decided good fortune to have evacuated the building successfully once already.

When we emerged from the building we picked up Chamberlain and paused to take our bearings before moving through the docks to the rendezvous where we were to report to Colonel Newman. As we hesitated I suddenly saw Chris Smalley and his small team run along the side of the old entrance down to the water's edge and there jump on board a motor launch which was getting under way (Burt's ML 262) stern first, towards the main stream of the river. As Smalley and his soldiers clambered on board, the ML came under heavy fire. I was vaguely conscious of their being caught in the fire of the German guns and thought 'Rather him than me, I hope they make it', but even as I turned to make my way through the docks I could see that the ML was already on fire and I was told later that it had exploded, killing most of those on board including Smalley.

Although I did not know it at that time, Burtenshaw was also already dead or dying at the other end of the dry-dock in his attempts to blow up the large caisson there. The gates were sufficiently damaged to make them inoperative for, although my old friend 'Bertie' Burtenshaw died, his efforts were completed by my own Troop Sergeant, Frank Carr, who took over as 'Bertie' fell. Sergeant Frank Carr, RE, of No 5 Commando, a regular soldier who was the senior NCO assisting Lieutenant Burtenshaw's and Lieutenant Brett's parties to destroy the large caisson at the far end of the dry-dock, told me many years later:

> After confirming that no further action was required to destroy the other side of the caisson, i.e. that all the charges had been

hung over the dock rail and into the water of the inner U-boat basin, we joined Mr Brett's party and helped them reinforce their explosives on the inner side of the caisson. They were already under attack when we arrived and had already suffered some casualties, including Mr Brett who was hit in an arm and a leg. We (ourselves) did not have to fight to get there, but we certainly did to stay there. We had been under attack already several times when we laid our first charges as we helped Brett's party and WL came under extremely heavy fire from the six Oerlikons on Flak Towers across the other side of the inner dock basin and from the ships lying in the Basin as well as from a tanker in the dry-dock. Also guns were firing at us from the east side of the dock. The fire became so heavy we were forced to take cover under the decking of the caisson. We then nipped on to the dockside to engage the tanker, but as we were armed only with pistols, you can imagine it was pretty ineffectual. But a protection party armed with tommy-guns, Bren and Lewis guns arrived and silenced the tanker's guns, and we returned to our task.

After checking to make sure our ring-main of cordtex to the various charges had not been damaged I tried to find Mr Burtenshaw. Sadly, during this attack and counter-attack he had already been wounded several times and must have been killed, for I never saw him again and was told he was lying dead in the shadow of a nearby dock wall.

It was at this time that I had to take over command of the two parties. We then had another attempt at opening a hatch into the inside of the huge hollow caisson, but without success. (The Germans had covered the surface with heavy wooden beams and covered them with tar and grit to make a road.)

Time was passing and we should have been ready to 'blow'. The fact that we could not complete the whole task caused us some concern and I realised that we would have to blow the underwater charges only. We again came under fire, and the withdrawal rocket was also fired so I decided to set off the charges.

I checked that the caisson was clear and removed the pins from the igniters. The resultant explosion seen from quite close by myself and Lance-Corporal Lemon was heavier than originally planned because we combined both sets of charges rather than waste the ones we couldn't lay inside the caisson. We could see the water boiling as a result of the explosion.

To check, I walked the caisson to estimate the damage. I could hear running water at both ends and realised that the caisson was badly damaged, probably enough to move it off its seating and make it useless.*

Of my memories of that night I will never forget looking at the skyline round our RV (rendezvous) – there were fires everywhere, even in the water. The poor old MLs; and my thoughts 'You're not going to put this little lot right in a hurry,' and then the quiet remark, I think by Major Copeland, 'Sorry! There's no transport, you'll have to walk home!'

And so of the three of us from No 5 Commando, I was the only surviving officer and, what is more, although I didn't realise it at the time, I was also one of only 17 officers still alive out of the original 39 Commando officers who had embarked on the raid.

As we made our way along the side of the old entrance immediately adjacent to the dry-dock we kept to the shadows of the dockside walls and once again marvelled at the fact that the German gunners, firing their quick-firing cannon and heavy artillery at the motor launches in the river, did not stop to see us running along the road below them. When, however, I came to a swing-bridge which we had to cross I decided to take no chances and I led my team under the bridge, swinging hand over hand along the bridge girders with our feet not far above the deep water of the high tide, but completely hidden from anyone looking down on to the bridge. When we got to the other side of the entrance we clambered up on to the road and dodged through the shadows to our rendezvous. Here we met Colonel Newman who, with his sorely depleted HQ staff, was calmly acknowledging our salutes and reports as to what had

* Of the two demolition parties of that caisson from No 5 and No 12 Commandos eight were killed: Lt Burtenshaw, Sgts Ide, Bainbridge, Fergusson; Cpls Chetwynd, Jones and Blount; and L/Cpl Stokes; and most of the rest were wounded, particularly Brett, who later died as a result of his wounds.

happened. So far so good. My only frustration at that time was that in jumping over a fence to cross the bridge my remaining Colt automatic pistol had snapped from its lanyard and skidded over the side of the dock into the water.

Other than my two grenades, I now had nothing with which to defend myself because Chamberlain had dropped the other pistol which I had given him in the pump-house. Many years later, after the war, the old French night-watchman in the dock told me that he had found an automatic pistol just where we had left Chamberlain to protect us whilst we were underground. I didn't tell the watchman we had decided, if we ran into him during the raid, that he would have to be shot for fear that he would hinder our operation!

I reported to Colonel Newman that the pumps had been destroyed. Cheerful as always, he smiled and told me to move along into the shadow of some railway trucks. Other teams were arriving either in small groups or in ones and twos. I remember seeing Gerard Brett limping badly, but with most of his team intact. Bill Etches was also hobbling by but he seemed also to have most of his team intact. Corran Purdon*, little more than a boy and the babe of the whole operation, appeared to be all right and then 'Micky' Burn walked in – but alone. We did not realise then that the rest of his team were mostly killed or drowned. He was, in fact, saved from drowning by Corporal Arthur Young, a Gordon Highlander, who, although already wounded, some-how swam Burn ashore and to safety.

And so, as we waited in among the railway trucks on the dockside, we were cheerful enough, although there was small-arms fire now all around us. No one seemed to be taking cover, although I thought at the time that one German grenade could have killed most of us.

There were some two or three dozen of us and others in the vicinity; there were also Germans everywhere – we could hear them shouting to each other. Then Colonel Newman and Major 'Bill' Copeland arrived.

* Now Major-General Corran Purdon MC.

Major W.O. 'Bill' Copeland, South Lancashire Regiment and No 2 Commando, second-in-command of the Commando force, was the oldest member of the entire force and a veteran of the First World War. He was in charge of all Commandos on *Campbeltown* and inspired us all with his calmness under the heavy fire, never once raising his voice and yet in complete control of our part of the raid, as Sergeant Carr also testifies.

We were all quite cheerful, or seemed to be so, but suddenly became very quiet when Newman said, 'Good heavens, Bill, surely those are ours' – 'those' being the burning wrecks of a number of MLs, our transport home. There was an extraordinary air of calmness at this point and one of almost complete confidence that somehow we would find a way home. But as more of our soldiers reported in from all directions in the dock area the situation began to look desperate. The enemy were virtually within yards of us but had not seen or realised where we were, sheltered as we were by the railway trucks. In anticipation of operating in such close quarters we had purposely whitened our webbing equipment as a means of identification and there were those who wore the kilt, an unmistakable identification. But it could only be a matter of time before the Germans discovered us if we were to stay there much longer and although we were ready to continue fighting, our main objective was to get away from the docks as fast as possible.

After a brief discussion between Newman and Copeland and an increasing realisation that our naval craft were either destroyed or had already left the scene in an endeavour to escape through the continuing heavy fire of the German coastal defences to the open sea, Newman decided that we must try and fight our way through and out of the dock area and the old town into the new town and away into the country, and there attempt to escape south through France and into Spain – just as Squadron Leader Evans had instructed us on board *PJC*.

Even at that stage of the action there seemed little concern – rather the contrary. We were, however, short of weapons and ammunition. Many of us were wounded; later we realised that over fifty per cent were wounded, but at that time it was not so obvious in the dark. And so we set forth in street-fighting formation, that is, moving in single file on each side of the street, one side covering the other as we advanced towards freedom. Those few who had tommy-guns and pistols led the way and Donald Roy of No 2 Commando, who had commanded the assault team that protected me at the pump-house, and 'Tiger' Watson, a young round-faced officer from The Black Watch and No 2 Commando, excelled themselves in leading the charge through the dockside streets towards the town. As we left the shelter of the trucks we had to recross the street running towards the U-boat pens and the giant inner Penhouet Dock basin. We dashed past the gaps between the cavernous ware-houses and, as I reached the other side of this street, Corran Purdon followed me, only to catch his foot in some wire and sprawl full length to a halt at my feet. We burst into laughter and hauled him to his feet, such was the atmosphere at that moment.

I didn't laugh for very long, however, for almost immediately I was hit again by a bullet, fired at us by one of the Germans retreating before our charge, and a bullet lodging in one's knee is a most painful way of stopping one's mobility. There was no way I could continue to run, or walk even, and I collapsed. 'Ron' Butler, one of my sergeants, would have none of this and with young Jimmy Brown, the Argyll and Sutherland High-lander from my Commando, they carried me until I realised that I was a hindrance to their own chances of escape and I ordered them to leave me. They were reluctant to do so, but recognised that they had little alternative.

I watched them run alongside the dock basin with the others until they reached the main bridge which connected the docks with the town. Despite the Germans' defensive fire, which by this time was increasing, and the noise of ricocheting bullets and the explosion of grenades, the Commandos slowly disappeared into the dark as they fought their way through the town.

I was alone. All I could do was hope for the best for there was nothing I could do but wait. Despite my predicament an even more frightening possibility threatened me. I was still very close to *Campbeltown* – wedged into the gate of the dry-dock and with five tons of ammonal explosive fused to explode and destroy the gate in a few hours' time.

No one else passed me as I lay there, for so quickly had the main party launched itself against the Germans that I was already in the rear of the force by the time Butler and Brown found me. As I now lay in the shadows of the warehouses on the wet, cobbled road and propped up against a cold, sweaty dock-side wall, I could see across the water of the Penhouet Dock basin straight into the giant U-boat pens – and they looked rather like a row of huge lock-up garages, only open and dark and wet.

6

Capture: Dead or Alive

I could hardly move because of the bullet lodged in my right leg. I tried again, and again, but it was impossible. I was stuck, helpless and immobile, where two of my soldiers had left me.

After I had lain on that road for an hour or more (it was about four o'clock in the morning), without sound or warning I was joined by a young British soldier. I did not know his name and, regrettably, I never asked it, but I recognised him as one of our soldiers from No 2 Commando.

The soldier and I lay silent. Then, at my suggestion, he bravely crawled from the shadows of the warehouse across the road to the dockside, and looked down at the water searching for a boat in which we could hide. There was no boat. There was nothing except the dark, grimy warehouses behind us, and railway trucks and Germans everywhere. We could hear them shouting to each other as they searched for those of us who were left behind and still alive.

Our main parties had already left on their desperate attempt to return home by sea; and others were trying to escape overland through France to Spain and freedom. As there were no boats we debated what to do. The soldier seemed to have a quiet faith in me, and little did he realise my own helplessness. His silent obedience gave me little time to feel fear; rather, I felt responsible for him. I tried to think of some means whereby we could crawl away and hide together until the fighting in the dockside battle died down and I could rest and regain some strength and mobility. But there was nothing we could do except lie there and wait for some miracle – like being picked up by the French. We had been told of the emergence by Squadron Leader Evans of an organised French resistance movement. But those were early days and resistance did not yet qualify for a capital R. Although the Frenchmen were there – all round us – they had little or no chance of helping us against the power of the German occupying forces.

Before we could do anything, however, the decision was brutally wrested from us for, suddenly, walking towards us were three Germans in black uniforms and steel helmets. I thought they were of the Waffen SS but, on later reflection, I wonder – they could have been naval or railway police in their black uniforms. No matter, they were hostile and they were armed – with Schmeisser machine pistols. We were not, for we – or that is I – had given my grenades to my escaping soldiers and my Colt automatic had fallen into dockside water some two hours previously.

The Germans were very jumpy and reacted violently when they saw us. Shouting and pointing their firearms they stopped a yard or so in front of us. I froze and told the soldier not to move.

To cut a few shattering seconds short – they shot him. He made little sound and fell to the ground. For, as they shouted 'Hände hoch' – a command which has a compulsive ring about it – the soldier ignored my whispers, slowly stood up, and immediately died.

They shot him at a range of a few feet only.

I could not move, and I lived.

When I failed to get up they bent down to lift me and, as they did so, they either saw my light khaki brown pips, the pips of a lieutenant, or realised that I was wounded. Still shouting into my face they nevertheless dragged me – quite a long way it seemed – a hundred yards or so along the dockside to a cross-road junction and into a small dark building, full of German soldiers and some other wounded Commandos.

To be fair, the three Germans who captured me laid me on the floor and propped me up against yet another wall – a luxury which I began to appreciate for it was more comfortable than lying flat on the ground with no support.

As well as the shock of seeing the soldier being shot I had another problem on my mind: I did not keep a diary during the war, although many there were who broke orders to do so, but I did have a small Kodak camera in one of the ammunition pouches of my webbing equipment. I knew that if the camera was found when daylight came, there on the film were exposures I had made showing us aboard *Campbeltown*, which, at that time, had been wearing a large German flag with its equally large swastika. How was I to destroy the film? Every time I so much as moved or twitched an eyelid the Germans pointed their rifles at me in a most menacing fashion. Suddenly, another soldier burst into our small room waving a short sword-type machete over his head and shouting and cursing at us. He then made some frighteningly close swipes at my face with the sword, but he was pulled away by our guards before he could do me or the others any harm. I suppose it could be called 'pride of ownership', for there was then a sharp exchange between our captors and the man with the sword and, after some noisy words, he was turned out into the street and told in no uncertain terms to go away.

This distracted our guards' attention and their preoccupation with the argument which ensued was just the opportunity I needed. In the excitement of the incident I quietly and surreptitiously opened the flap of my ammunition pouch and, feeling into its recess, I opened the little catch of the camera so that when it was moved it would spring open and spoil the film. I did not try to do this myself, let alone move the camera, for had I done so I would have been seen. I never knew what happened to my camera for, when daylight dawned and the Germans took the rest of my equipment away from me, they didn't even look into the ammunition pouches, let alone find the camera.

But where had the short sword come from? It was carried by one of our assault troops; for in those early days of the war it was given to our tommy-gunners as a replacement for the bayonet. They may have been a novelty then, but they were no different from the original Roman short swords and were really no reason for the Germans to get so excited.

Typical of what happened to the others is the story of Lance-Sergeant 'Dick' Bradley, of the Royal Berkshire Regiment, who was German-born and had been educated in southern Germany: 'During the attack I was badly wounded,' he told me. 'A bullet landed in my chest, went through the lung and came out at the side (of my body) below my shoulder-blade. I gradually lost consciousness. After a while, maybe an hour, I became half-conscious. Two Commandos passed by, near me, one saying to the other, "Oh, he's a goner." In my half-sleepy state I agreed with them. Later I heard two Germans saying to each other, "I'm going to let him have a bullet in case he's playing a trick on us." The other said, "Leave him alone, he's dead." I don't think I have ever kept so still and silent in my life.'

Lieutenant The Hon. 'Micky' Wynn was on board MTB 74 on the way down the River Loire: 'As we proceeded downriver at full speed, little did we realise that the German shore batteries had picked us up, but owing to the speed of our vessel (40 knots) it seemed as though they were firing astern of us. However when we were threequarters down the estuary we saw two of our chaps off one of the MLs on a Carley float, and they were directly ahead of us. One had to make a snap decision. Either we stopped, which we could do very quickly, or we went on which would have meant that they would have been washed off their Carley float and drowned. It was an awful decision to make as we had twenty-six survivors we had picked up, ten of our own crew, and yet it would have always been very much on our mind if we had washed those chaps off the Carley float for them to drown. So I decided to stop the vessel and we pulled up right alongside them. My crew had got hold of them, but unfortunately at that very moment the German shore batteries found their mark and two shells went straight through us. I was blown from the bridge down into the bilges; my chief motor mechanic, Bill Lovegrove, before jumping over the side, decided to come down into the bilges to see if he could find me. He put his arm round me and pulled me up on deck and jumped over the side with me, and kept hold of me, and swam with me to the Carley float which everybody was trying to hang onto. Those who did make it to the Carley float, owing to the very intense cold of the sea, gradually let go and drifted off until there were only three of us left out of thirty-six.'

Commander Ryder summed up this aspect of the raid when he wrote in his book: 'The gallantry and desperation of the fighting of the crews manning the small coastal craft (eighteen of them) in the action on the River Loire that night forms one of the greatest chapters of fighting at sea during the last war.

'Few of them survived and the destruction wrought on them by the intense German defences has never really been fully appreciated, even today. That some of these vessels escaped and made their way back to England is a miracle and another story. Without these men's bravery and tenacity it must be remembered that the raid on St Nazaire could never have succeeded, for *Campbeltown*, on her own, would have had to absorb the combined weight of fire of some ninety medium and heavy coastal and ack-ack guns firing over open sites, in addition to numerous lethal automatic cannon and machine-guns.'

In our temporary prison there was another young soldier, a Cameron Highlander, who was wearing the kilt. Half of his head had been blown off and, as he sat with his face clasped in his arms, he made the most horrible gurgling noises. When daylight came he was still alive but covered in blood and when the German army photographers arrived to photograph us they concentrated on him. Later his photograph was published all over the world to show what had happened to the British in 'their disastrous raid' on St Nazaire. But despite Germany's propaganda claims that we had failed – and that for some time High Command back in London thought we had failed – we had, in fact, succeeded.

Although it happened later than intended *Campbeltown* exploded as planned, and her five tons of ammonal blew the giant caisson off its sill and rendered the dock completely useless for the rest of the war, and in so doing it killed

300–400 German onlookers – troops and sailors.

The pumping-station with its four huge impeller pumps had already been destroyed, the machinery of the two winding stations had both been blown into little pieces. Finally, the far caisson, although not blown completely off its sill, was rendered useless by well-placed explosive charges all along and below its high-water mark.

Two days later, when the Germans thought the action was finished, the torpedoes which had been fired by MTB 74 into the gates of the dock entrance exploded under water and blew the caisson gates into useless scrap-iron.

As dawn came we were taken from our little room, which we then realised was, in fact, a small dockside café, and laid on the pavement on the street outside. For the next hour or more we were the subject of much curiosity and photographing by our captors – German soldiers in their green and grey uniforms and sailors in the dark blue jackets and white trousers of U-boat crews of the Kriegsmarine.

It is only recently that some photographs from this time have been found. They show us, the survivors, as we were discovered in the docks, some miraculously still alive as they were hauled out of the ebbing tide of the River Loire and those who were captured far out to sea as they tried to escape back to Britain.

The photograph of my group (see Plate 13) shows Gerard Brett of the Royal Ulster Rifles (shot in the legs), 'Tiger' Watson of The Black Watch (shot in the chest), Sgt 'Dick' Bradley, Private J. McCormack, and myself in my tin hat. One particular photograph shows me being carried away, in between two soldiers, before they dumped me into a dirty old camouflaged army truck with a wooden burner for fuel and an open top. An old bone-rattler if ever there was one!

Time was ticking by but nothing we could do hastened our departure, for if we did express concern we would reveal the secret in *Campbeltown*. However, still hiding our anxiety and fears we were finally trundled out of the old port, past the

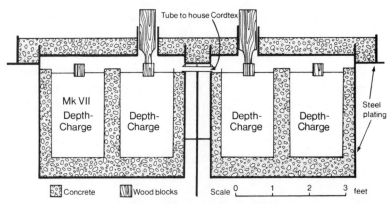

Fig. 4 A cross-section of *Campbeltown*'s explosive charges. There were six similar sections, made up from twenty-four depth-charges making a total of five tons of ammonal blasting powder. Enclosed in steel compartments, and lined in concrete to withstand shock, the charges were connected to a large ring-main of cordtex instantaneous fuse. This was, in turn, attached to delayed-action fuses timed to explode several hours after arrival

U-boat pens, through the town out into the country and along the coast road. A few miles northward and we entered a sprawling seaside town, La Baule, which became our home for the next few days and a temporary hospital for us.

When I look at those old photographs I find it difficult to recapture the feeling of apprehension which we felt before leaving St Nazaire, for, to those of us who were members of the demolition teams, there was not only the anxious waiting, but the knowledge that only a hundred yards away our flagship, HMS *Campbeltown*, still jammed into the gates of the dry-dock, had hidden in her hull below decks five tons of ammonal timed to explode shortly. That was why I had kept my tin hat on. Ammonal was the black blasting powder used during the war for mining and as the contents of sea-mines. HMS *Campbeltown*'s charges were timed to explode at about 05.30 hours but did not in fact 'blow' until 11.35 hours (local time) with a gigantic explosion.

But the feeling of apprehension, the excitement and the nervous reactions of our German guards gave us little opportunity to think of anything but the immediate present and of those who lay alongside us, some of whom were dying. Indeed it was not until two days after the tense and exciting events of that morning that we came 'back to earth' and began to take an interest in our surroundings in the Hôtel l'Hermitage at La Baule.

7

The Legend of St Nazaire

Apart from our guards, still in their steel helmets and armed with rifles, patrolling between our mattress beds on the floor, there were the Kriegsmarine nurses and two or three civilian nurses: kind, French, middle-aged ladies. The guards still would not allow any talking, but whisper we did.

By process of elimination the French nurses discovered that a few of us could understand French – Gerard Brett, whose French and German were quite good, and myself, not so good; but the months I had spent in France before Dunkirk had given me a fluency of a kind. There were a few others – but no more than half a dozen out of the hundred lying there in that makeshift hospital at La Baule could understand any foreign language.

We had little inclination to chatter, let alone in French, and so perhaps it was all the more significant when the French-women started to whisper to us about the recent hours and events at St Nazaire. Apart from telling us what we already knew, they kept referring to the explosion of *Campbeltown* – only they did not know it was called that at that time – and that when the ship had blown up many Germans had been killed, and some British soldiers too.

When the explosion took place several of our people were still in the dockside area, being questioned or given medical treatment; but there was no one at the time who had a direct view of what happened. Commander Beattie himself was perhaps one of the nearest for having been picked up at sea by a German torpedo-boat, *Jaguar*, he was, at the very moment of the explosion, in St Nazaire being politely interrogated by a German officer who spoke good English. Suddenly the glass from the window of the room in which they were sitting crashed to the floor and the whole town seemed to shake with a thunderous explosion. Beattie realised that it must have been *Campbeltown* but he did not reveal at that time his contribution to that explosion.

The whispered reports from our nurses about British soldiers were puzzling and we whispered back for more details; but our guard became suspicious and the nurses were ordered away. We waited for the guards to change and then questioned the French ladies again. They were insistent that their information was correct and that the Germans were talking about the incident among themselves all the time. They also told us that there had been more fighting the next two days following further heavy explosions.

Bit by bit they described a picture of continuing chaos which had lasted for several hours after we were captured. They described how, when the ship blew up, hundreds.of Germans were in the wrecked ship, no doubt looking for souvenirs and chocolate, as well as some British officers – all of whom were blown to bits. They also said that there were several more German soldiers on the dockside nearby who took the full force of the five-ton blast. That was what I had feared would happen to us earlier during the few hours before we were captured.

How, we asked, did they, the French, know of this? We knew the German guards were very jumpy but we had no way of knowing the reason why.

The French nurses replied that their friends in St Nazaire had passed the word to them to tell us, no doubt in an attempt to reassure us and maybe even to help get word back to Britain.

At first we were sceptical: it all seemed too good to be true and we could not believe the Germans would have been so careless. By their very nature they were always suspicious, and their approach to problems was methodical and cautious. But photographs taken of *Campbeltown* before the explosion show now that there were numerous Germans standing around taking their eternal photographs, seemingly unconcerned, and confident that there was nothing left to fear from the wreck of the ship.

But how were there British officers or soldiers also on the ship? If so, were they acting as self-appointed decoys? Or were they under duress to reveal to the Germans the real reason for the ship's ramming the dry-dock gate? The nurses insisted that the British were officers, but there was little to identify us, soldier from officer, except for the small cloth pips officers wore on their shoulders – for we had learnt long ago that an officer's identity, and collar and tie, was a sure and priority target for the enemy.

Could a German, in fact, have left the docks before the explosion and lived to report the true facts to his superiors? We will never know, but the legend lives on.

No matter their rank, if Commandos were on the ship they would have known of the secret hidden explosives – but nothing more. Captain Bob Montgomery, the young sapper from the Special Service Brigade, has since confirmed that the explosive in *Campbeltown* was the responsibility of the Navy and Lt Tibbets RN was in charge of placing the five tons of ammonal, made up of twenty-four 400-lb depth-charges encased in concrete, in the hold of the ship. Tibbets was also in charge of setting the eight types of fuse which he himself had primed a few hours before we arrived at St Nazaire.

There was no one else in the raiding force who knew the actual details and it would have required the highest technical knowledge to trace the complex wiring to defuse the detonators, even if they were found. It would have been a virtual impossibility to have so defused a set of twenty-four 400-lb depth-charges connected in this way in the time between dawn light and 11.35 (local time) when the ship actually exploded some six hours later than planned.

Tibbets was killed at sea, trying to escape with the remainder of *Campbeltown*'s crew who had been embarked on ML 177, and the only other person who could have coped with such a complexity of explosives would have been Bill Pritchard, the

Royal Engineer Officer from the Special Service Brigade attached to our force and in charge of those of us in the demolition teams.

For a long time afterwards it was thought that Pritchard had sacrificed himself for the success of the raid. He did pay the supreme price, but he was killed elsewhere and his body lies buried with the rest of our dead at Escoublac, some ten miles north of St Nazaire; and there is a British War Graves Commission headstone which marks his resting-place. If he had been aboard *Campbeltown* he would have been blown to pieces with the hundreds of others and therefore would have been unrecognisable.

There has always been some doubt about the number of casualties caused by the explosion both on the ship and on the dock alongside. The German figure has never been annotated satisfactorily. Sadly their claims or admissions varied with their propaganda at the time. If they won an action, casualties favoured their story; if they were defeated, their losses were minimised. In this case we had inflicted a lethal blow to their then seeming infallibility, and, much to their surprise, they had been caught badly off guard.

The only objective and possibly reliable claim to be considered is that of the French. A letter written to me in 1952 by Le Contre-Amiral Lepotier, Chief of Staff of the 2nd Maritime Region, Port of Brest, concludes, after extensive inquiries, that 60 German officers (including high-ranking officers) and 300 other ranks were killed by the explosion of *Campbeltown*. Reports at the time describe the fearful carnage with blood everywhere, and pieces of flesh and bits of body hanging from ruined buildings. Also reported was the dreadful task for the German soldiers of cleaning up the remains of the hundreds of bodies before the French workers could be persuaded to go to more serious work repairing vital dock installations.

And so we come back to the question: who was it who lured the Germans to their deaths?

We will never know – but one thing is certain: our French

nurses were adamant about the accuracy of their information and they were the only contact with those of us who were left behind in the area – we, the only survivors at nearby La Baule, guarded day and night and completely cut off from all other possible means of contact from the outside world except for our German guards. Those of our party who had not been wounded were already on their way to Germany and were hundreds of miles away and, although they heard of this report months later, they had little or no knowledge of what happened at St Nazaire after they were captured and driven away from the docks to imprisonment.

Facts are always hard to identify in the confusion of war and all too often the cynic's voice gets an ill-deserved hearing, particularly so from those who were not even at or near the scene of the action. Recent histories of the Second World War and other wars since tend to discredit rather than accept the reports of those who were there and who survived, for the cynics find it easy to disprove reports which by the very nature of wartime action would often be incomplete because of the deaths and casualties resulting from the fighting.

For fear of contradiction and of the disbelief of the eternal cynic I can only write what I heard those French nurses tell us at La Baule in the German POW hospital. Their report has remained unchallenged and as the wartime resistance movement grew in France, so the story of St Nazaire became a symbol of hope and of the victory to come. As the President of France, M Ramadier, said after the war 'You were the first to give us hope.'

One hundred and sixty-nine British officers and men were killed at St Nazaire on the morning of 28 March 1942 – out of a total of 611 naval and military personnel including two Australian, two New Zealand and three Canadian naval officers who went up the River Loire to attack St Nazaire, and of the sixteen demolition officers eight were dead. Not all of them were found or seen as they died and many there were who were drowned as they were wounded and swept out to sea in the tidal

races of that great river. In addition over 200 were wounded
and captured, while five walked away from the scene through
France to Spain.

One fact remains unchallenged however: *Campbeltown* did
explode as planned, albeit some six hours later than intended,
and in so doing killed many more Germans than we could
possibly have hoped for and two days later two torpedoes fired
by 'Micky' Wynn from MTB 74 exploded, leading to further
victory for us and death to the enemy and, sadly and accidentally, for many Frenchmen too. Against such facts – known facts
– I prefer to believe the French nurses in our temporary hospital
in the Hôtel l'Hermitage at La Baule. Facts there were, the rest
perhaps part legend – particularly so to the French of those
wartime years.

1 Irregular Warfare Training Centre, Lochailort, in the western Highlands of Scotland, where Commandos were trained from 1940 to 1942, until the Commando Training Centre was formed at Achnacarry nearby

2 Every Commando soldier had to be able to swim and No 4 Troop, No 5 Commando, are seen here after swimming at Falmouth, 1941. SC-S (*first on left*) in charge; Sgt Frank Carr DCM, who took over from wounded and dead officers at St Nazaire, is at the end of back row in swimming trunks

3 HMS *Princess Josephine Charlotte*, an ex-cross-Channel ferry, converted to a Commando troop-carrier, the floating home of the Commandos who attacked St Nazaire

4 ML 446 alongside HMS *Princess Josephine Charlotte*, anchored in the Carrick Roads, Falmouth, being loaded with troops and stores for the raid, 26 March 1942. ML 446 escaped after the raid out to sea, but unfortunately had to be scuttled

5 The dock area of St Nazaire lies some 6 miles up the River Loire. The dry-dock, then the largest in the world, is on the right of the photo running diagonally from river to inland basin, which is open to the river at high tide

6 HMS *Campbeltown* during her conversion; two of her four funnels were removed and the other two cut back on a slant to make her look like a German Möwe class torpedo-boat

7 Forward of the bridge a 12-pounder quick-firing, high-angle gun was fitted; and the bridge structure was encased in 10-lb NMBP plating which protected Cdr Beattie and his crew from intensive German gunfire

8 MTB 74, with Lt 'Micky' Wynn at the wheel. The MTB was then one of the fastest
craft in the Royal Navy with a speed in excess of 40 knots

9 HMS *Sturgeon*, an 'S'-class submarine and the rendezvous ship for Operation
CHARIOT forces, as it approached St Nazaire at midnight on 27 March 1942

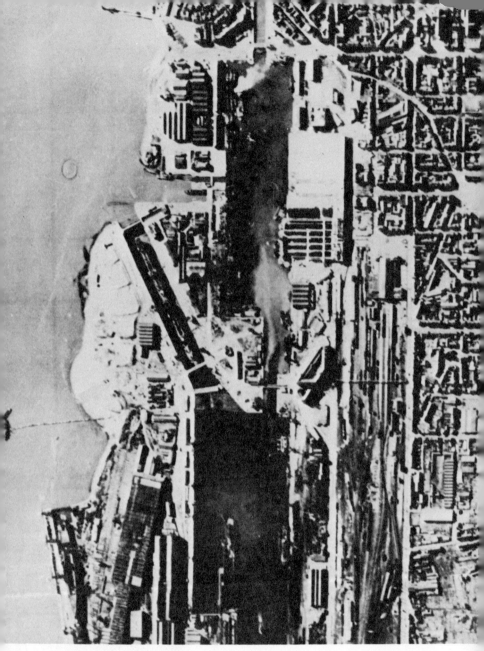

10 Aerial photo of St Nazaire, taken shortly before the raid, with two large merchant ships in the dry-dock

11 HMS *Campbeltown*, wedged into the outer caisson of the dry-dock, shortly before she exploded and blew the caisson off its rollers, exposing the dock basin to the powerful ebb and flow of the sea and the River Loire

12 Survivors from ML 306 being brought ashore at St Nazaire after surrendering at sea to German torpedo-boat *Jaguar*; (*l-r*): Sub-Lt Philip Dark, OS Ralph Batteson, Cpl Glyn Salisbury, Lt R. O. C. Swayne MC, No 1 Commando, and, behind him, Sub-Lt P. W. Landy RANVR

13 Wounded and prisoners, early in the morning after the raid (*top to bottom*): Sgt 'Dick' Bradley, No 2 Commando; SC-S, No 5 Commando; Pte J. McCormack, No 2 Commando, who died a few days later; Lt W. H. 'Tiger' Watson, No 2 Commando; and Lt G. Brett, No 12 Commando

14 German troops clearing the dock area after the fighting, and passing a dead Commando, Sgt G. Ide, Royal Corps of Signals and No 5 Commando

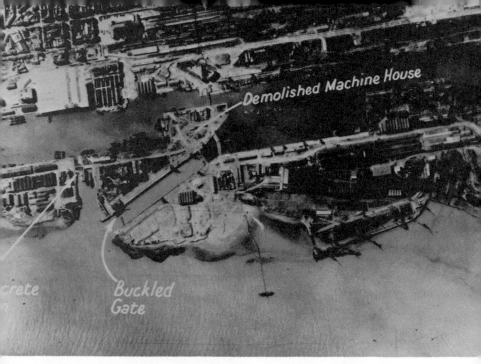

Demolished Machine House

Buckled Gate

crete

15 Aerial photo of the dry-dock, a few days after the raid, showing that the caisson has disappeared and that other damage has been done; the dry-dock is full of water at high tide

16 Nine months later, the Germans have filled in the entrance to the dry-dock basin. Circled is the stern of HMS *Campbeltown*, some 500ft into the dock where she was swept after she exploded

17 SC-S's KennKarte (POW ID card), dated 15 August 1942, when he arrived in Germany at Oflag IX AH Hauptlager ('top camp')

Kr.-Gef. Offizierlager IX A

Hauptlager

Zweiglager   am   15.8.   194

Kennkarte für Kriegsgefangene

Nur gültig für den Lagerbetrieb und in Verbindung mit de

Erk.-Marke Nr. 18784 Frontst.

Dienstgrad: Leutnant

Nama: Chant

Vorname: Stuart, Whitmore

Lichtbild

Zur Beachtung!

Die Kennkarte dient als
weis der Krf. gegenüber
Organen der deutschen La
kommandantur. Sie ist wie
Erk.-Marke stets mitzufü
u, mit dieser auf Verlange
namentlichen Appells und
Verlassen des Lagers ve
weisen.

Verlust ist sofort zu me

Der Komma

18 Some of the Commando soldiers in Stalag 383, Bavaria, in Germany. SC-S's own Sergeants Ron Butler MM, from No 1 Commando (*centre middle row*); W. Chamberlain (*right middle row*); and A. W. King (*second from left, back row*)

19 Courtyard of Oflag IX AH ('top camp') at Spangenberg, known as a Senior
Officers' camp, where SC-S and others were sent for security reasons. No one ever
escaped from this old castle during the Second World War

20 Oflag IX AZ at Rotenburg-am-Fulda, where a tunnel was successfully dug – only
to be betrayed in 1943. The building on the right-hand side of the photo is where
the tunnel began

21 Lt-Colonel A. C. Newman VC, Military Commander

22 Lt-Commander S. H. Beattie VC RN, Commanding Officer of HMS *Campbeltown*

23 Commander R. E. D. Ryder VC RN, Naval Force Commander

24 Able Seaman W. A. Savage VC RN, pom-pom gunlayer of MGB 314 (posthumous)

25 Sergeant T. F. Durrant VC RE, No 1 Commando (posthumous) – the only soldier to win a VC in the war fighting in a naval action on ML 306

8

POW Life Begins

As a prisoner-of-war I started my captivity lying on the marble floor of the Hôtel l'Hermitage in La Baule, still today one of the best hotels in France. La Baule, 16 km north of St Nazaire, faces the sea with its stiff breezes and surf rolling in from the Atlantic. It was, and still is, very fashionable. Prosperous upper-class French families send their children there in summer for its bracing air as distinct from the heat of the Midi in the south where the bulk of the French go every summer for their holidays.

There were over one hundred of us wounded lying in that hotel hospital in addition to a considerable number of wounded Germans. Still wearing our uniforms and heavy Commando boots, we lay on mattresses covered in coats and grey army blankets. Our nurses were German sailors, with a few French-women. The sailors were smart, in white hospital jackets and trousers tucked into black jackboots. This always seemed strange to me, but during captivity I rarely saw a German in any footwear other than jackboots.

The first day in captivity was traumatic and it is clearly and indelibly etched on my memory. As other wounded were brought in, in ones and twos, we began to look for our friends, and our own soldiers, and the sailors looked for their shipmates.

I was lying between a naval lieutenant and a Commando sergeant, and next to him was Gerard Brett. The sailor was aptly named G.E.A. Barham, a sub-lieutenant of ML 457, and the sergeant was called Alf Searson, of the Royal Sussex Regiment and No 2 Commando. Brett became a great personal friend. As we whispered to each other, German sentries patrolled between us, ordering us to keep quiet. But by then we were in various stages of exhaustion and semi-consciousness and we did not need much telling. Some form of order was eventually established and the long and weary process of operating, and bandaging, began. The German wounded were dealt with first and it was not until the late evening that the German doctors began to operate on us.

I have little memory of that day-long wait, except the glass of lemonade (or was it barley water?) that I was given – the most delicious drink I ever remember – but the only one, for German hospitality was rapidly reduced to water. I don't recall that we had any food that first day, but that glass of lemonade will always remain one of the high spots of my stay in prison.

At some time or other during the day they took away our clothes and, worse, they took away our heavy Commando boots. We were very proud of those boots. They were the first such boots issued to the British army in the war; they were called *Souliers Vibran*, with heavy rubber soles, non-slip and silent in action. I often wonder what the Germans did with one hundred pairs of boots in an army numbering several million, all of whom wore jackboots.

We were not looking forward to the operating room, but we wanted to get it over with. All that day we waited. The sentries were changed every hour or so, and the nurses moved quietly among us taking our temperatures and doing the normal distasteful things required of every nurse. We had the odd visitors – civilians who wore Red Cross armbands and who tried to question us: they got little response. It was a case of name, rank and number and nothing much else.

I especially recall that unusual day, because it was similar to other hospital scenes I witnessed later that year, both in France and later in Germany – the same smells and the same timeless passage of days. During that first day of captivity, 28 March 1942, all that mattered was that I was alive – many of my friends were not.

At about nine o'clock in the evening they came for me, and lifted me on to a stretcher and carried me to another part of the except that it immediately became evident that a prisoner's diet was far different from the British army rations, not to mention the marvellous food on 'HM' ships in which we had been living for several days before the raid. The basic hospital menu consisted of a cup of acorn coffee, no sugar, no milk; and a slice of black bread for breakfast; a bowl of soup and another slice of bread for lunchtime and the same again for supper. Somewhere around mid-afternoon we had another drink, only this time of tisane. Not one of us had ever heard of tisane, and not many of us had tasted German bread before. Tisane is a type of herbal hot drink, still very popular in France but nothing compared with our Service cups of 'char', strong and hot. The bread was heavy, and we suspected sawdust to be one of the main ingredients. Heavy and filling, it became our staple diet. Later when we were moved to Germany and received Red Cross parcels, we spread our meagre margarine and jam on it, to make a good meal. But *then* there was no butter or jam.

Our hunger was never satisfied and we dreamt of our favourite meals. I used to dream of cream cakes, although I never really liked cream cakes, but dream I did. I slept through nightmares every night and two or three days after capture I had a vivid dream of dining in the Angel Hotel in Cardiff where we had very recently been training, in the Barry Docks. That dream dinner was a wartime meal, but I savoured every mouthful and enjoyed the company of my friends. I particularly remembered Ronnie Swayne of the Herefordshire Regiment and No 1 Commando*, a tall young man from Shropshire, just down from Oxford, who had his young wife Charmian with him. They had been married only a few months. Ronnie had a bull terrier called Lou which he took everywhere with him. We were sitting on benches in a cosy room with subdued lighting and we were enjoying ourselves. It was all so clear that I did not believe life could be so cruel as to wake me and have me back in a prison hospital. That really was one of the most depressing

* Now Sir Ronald Swayne MC, a pioneer of the container ship.

incidents of those early days. After that I tried to induce similar hallucinations when I dozed off to sleep each night, but never could I match that dinner of dreams in Cardiff. Later, when I became interpreter for the soldiers and sailors with me, I used to dream in French – the only time I became so fluent, even when I lived in France after the war.

Altogether we were about one hundred strong, all quite young, and as a lieutenant I was equal in rank with the handful of other naval and army officers, wounded like myself; but I could speak French.

I mention seniority, because in captivity we were in effect all equal, all wounded, all lying on German naval mattresses, and all eating the same food. There were occasions, however, when the Germans would consult with us, the officers, to ask our help in translations and explanations. I cannot recall any conversations of significance that first week, partly because the Germans at first forbade us to talk at all, and principally because we were all suffering varying degrees of shock at being prisoners, and from the effects of our wounds. One example, however, will always stick in my memory: one of our sergeants, Alf Searson, was lying near me. To my amazement he was on his feet a few days after capture; swathed in bandages round his chest, whiter in the face than I have ever seen anyone before, and telling me that he could not live long because he had been shot in the lungs.

I tended to believe him but told him to shut up; at least he could walk, and I couldn't. The incredible thing is that I was right, and he was wrong, for he recovered quickly and was soon sent off to Germany, from where he and two others of our party escaped in one of the most dramatic and audacious escapes of the war. Having been recaptured after three attempts they retraced their steps back from their escape attempt to the Swiss frontier – to a POW camp in Poland (Gross-Zeidel). From there, on their fourth attempt, they took a train again and were successful in crossing the frontier at Schaffhausen to Switzerland and to freedom. Searson was with Lance-Sergeant 'Dick'

Bradley, Royal Berkshire Regiment and No 2 Commando, who, with his fluent German and knowledge of that part of Germany, acted as leader of the party including young Private Jimmy Brown of the Argyll and Sutherland Highlanders and No 5 Commando, who had helped to carry me when I was wounded the second time.★

Then there was the sickening sight of the naval sub-lieutenant, Barham, who smuggled a scalpel from a nurse's trolley to operate on himself – on his scrotum – removing small pieces of shrapnel which he had not dared tell the German doctors about, for fear of their reaction. Anyway, it started me thinking, for I, too, had several pieces of metal still scattered about in my legs, hands, face and in my scrotum, or so I thought. But I was not as tough as Barham, and said nothing. It was not until several weeks later when French doctors and nurses, themselves prisoners, took us into their care, that my fears were confirmed, but happily with no ill effects in the years that lay ahead. But then it was Lieutenant Veilleux, the French surgeon, who, with a slight degree of malice, said: 'Pour vous, mon Lieutenant, l'amour c'est fini.' Now, years later, father of three children, and a grandfather, I am happy to say that despite those painful days in hospital he was wrong.

★ He is now Professor Jim Brown, recent Head of the Department of Petroleum Engineering at Heriot-Watt University in Edinburgh.

9

Rennes

Easter Saturday 1942 was warm and a continuation of the lovely weather we had left behind us in Falmouth over a week before and which had made our sea voyage of thirty-six hours to St Nazaire so uneventful and comfortable. There was nothing particularly different about that Saturday morning, just the same hospital routine as we looked out of the hotel windows on to the calm grey waters of the Atlantic.

One learns quickly in prison, however; life, even if dull, was always full of surprises, and the Hôtel l'Hermitage suddenly changed from the calm routine we had come to expect to noise and shouting.

Germans did not move themselves about without making a lot of noise. Not understanding them then, most of us interpreted their aggressive movements and shouting as purposely directed at us, to impress their superiority over us, their prisoners. And they lost no opportunity of rubbing it in. It was, I suppose, a natural reaction, but they never seemed to realise that we were not impressed. The more they shouted the more we laughed – except, that is, when they started pointing their rifles at us. Then we stopped laughing.

The hustle and bustle increased, the shouting grew louder and we were on the move again. German soldiers were everywhere and our sailor nurses carried us on stretchers out into the waiting trucks. Only this time the trucks had canvas tops, so we could not see where we were going. A pity, for La Baule is very attractive with its smart hotels and its casino, its open squares and with some of the loveliest beaches in France, 7 km of them and ideal for children. But we could see none of this as the trucks rolled through empty streets to the railway station where we were to be put on a train.

The trains on the Continent were huge compared to our neat and smaller British rolling-stock, and their platforms were much lower. So moving our stretchers constituted quite a problem for the stretcher-bearers. Performing contortions of strength they succeeded, however, in lifting us up into the carriages of a hospital train, where we were to lie all day.

On reflection we came to appreciate the treatment we received then, and we realised later that it was because of the German naval base at St Nazaire. For St Nazaire was an exclusive place then, with its importance as a No 1 U-boat base. The German facilities in the hospital, the sailor nurses in their smart white uniforms, and the hospital train were really for their own sailors in the event that they were brought back from sea in need of medical attention. Although food was short, it was well cooked. The linen on our mattress beds really was clean. The nurses, mostly sailors, were also clean, and efficient, if, at times, such as in the blood and carnage of the operating room, hard, but still attentive. Also we were treated with a degree of respect, and of sympathy even. The shouting, whenever it did erupt, came from our soldier guards whom we had already learnt to despise for their stupid posturing.

We were shunted about quite a bit that Saturday, but I remember little of it, except that we lay for a long time in railway sidings and stations. At one particular station we stared out of our tightly closed windows at French civilians waiting for their Easter holiday trains. Our German guards were everywhere and the French were not very communicative. But every now and then they would make a V sign with their fingers, rubbing them up and down on the side of their noses. Some of them even made the dramatic hangman's sign; drawing their forefingers quickly across their throats and then jerking their heads back, and up, they made the sinister imitation of the hangman and his rope. We signalled back with our thumbs-up sign, but the French hangman's sign was perhaps the most symptomatic of those war years, and one of their gestures of defiance at that time. In any event it was of comfort to us, grim though it seems – comfort to know that we were among friends, although how they knew we were British soldiers, lying there in our shirts, we will never know.

That day was long and tiring – and hot – for the weather was still unusually warm. Although it is only 100 km from La Baule to Rennes it was not until dark that we arrived in the ancient capital city of Brittany.

To be carried out of the train and into the cool night air was a blessed relief; but shock rather than surprise was to be our next reaction. For suddenly, standing over us, and looking down from what seemed like an enormous height, was a giant of a man with a black face, made all the blacker by his white hospital overalls and white skull-cap. But he was smiling, with a beaming face and teeth like white rocks, and he seemed friendly, though rather scaring.

Bending down with another smaller man – an Arab – they lifted us up one by one as if we were small children, and gently placed us in ambulances. I say gently, for they were very gentle. And they were quiet, as distinct from the Germans, although there was a lot of chat. At first I couldn't understand, but as I listened I made out the odd word of French by the black man spoken with a deep grunting type of accent. Who were they? They weren't French, and what did they have to do with France, and Rennes in particular? The smaller man spoke with a different pitch and a coughing intonation. But they seemed to understand each other, and worked well together, as they filled up a small convoy of ambulances.

After a short journey at speed through quiet, empty streets, we stopped and, as the ambulance doors were opened, we could see we were outside a large building with a little light showing through the blackout curtains. We were carried into the building up some iron staircases and into a small whitewashed room with two rows of iron beds facing each other. We were at the end of the second stage of our journey. But where were we? Who were these black and brown men? There were many of them, with all shades of black and brown skins, and we assumed them to be nurses of some kind. Suddenly a German entered the room: he was a sergeant, neat and with close-cropped hair, dressed in a very smart uniform jacket and trousers with the silver chevrons of his rank on his shoulders and a medal ribbon in the top buttonhole of his jacket. He told us in French – and he spoke it well – that we were in a prisoner-of-war hospital, we were to obey his orders, and he in turn would do his best to see that we were cared for. Our nurse was to be the black giant; his name was Naboussin, Caporal Médecin of the French Colonial Army.

So that was it. We were in a prison hospital for French colonial soldiers who had been captured after the Fall of France in 1940. We were told later that there were some 20,000 colonial soldiers in the Rennes area, working on farms, in factories and being treated in this hospital. Many of them were very sick, and some were dying from the bad food and the effects of the two cold winters in captivity. They were mostly reservist soldiers, who had been called to the French colours as part of the French Colonial Army and who, when war came in 1939, were mobilised into service again, to fight for France and her Empire.

In a report by the International Red Cross our hospital was described as follows: 'This lazaret [hospital] which is established in the town of Rennes is in the old Senior Secondary School which was a boarding school . . .' Front-Stalag 133.

They were men from all over the world, from Algiers and Morocco in North Africa, from the Sudan and other French colonies on the African continent, from Madagascar, from the West Indies and Indo-China. We were told after the war that not many of them survived the war, for disease and European winters were too much for them and Naboussin, it was reported, died in France. It wasn't really the fault of our captors; it was too cold for these men from the tropics.

As prisoners we had a common bond, no matter that we were white and they were black. The nurses became the centre of our lives for we had no contact with the outside world. On that first day after our arrival – Easter Sunday – the heavy bells were sounding from the nearby Eglise Nôtre-Dame. The bells so filled our ward all that morning that it seemed at times as if we were in the bell loft itself. Ever since that Easter I have always preferred the church bells of France to the English clarion, so clear and beautiful, but somehow too high-pitched, and emasculated even. Finely tuned maybe, and with more variation they somehow lack the medieval grandeur of France. Maybe it still strikes a chord of remembrance in my Huguenot soul, for I have never forgotten the sounds and music of that Easter Sunday in Rennes. When I lived in Paris years later it was still there in the beauty and sound of Nôtre-Dame; as well as countless old churches all over France.

According to a report by the International Red Cross some two years later, the camp by then had accumulated just over forty books in various languages, some English. We had no paper, no pens or pencils. There were no wirelesses – we had nothing but our own company and freedom only to talk and wait for the next day. Life in the Rennes prison was very much the same as at La Baule except that life was more fundamental. The food, if anything, was worse and we no longer benefited from the hospitality of the German navy, such as it was. Life was not much above starvation-level – nor was it very clean and the medical facilities were rough and ready. The reason for this was, I suppose, the Germans' basic lack of respect for their French colonial captives. They were part of a defeated army, soldiers of what had been one of the largest armies in the world, now no more.

The Senegalese, of whom Naboussin was one, were different, however, and were hated by the Germans, for they had been one of the most feared soldiers of the First World War and in the fighting in 1940. Their terrible high-pitched cry of 'Coup, coup', which they yelled when attacking with a bayonet, struck terror in the ears of the German soldier. But here in prison the Senegalese were at the mercy of the Germans, and many of them suffered accordingly.

Many were their stories, but the one we liked best concerned Naboussin. When he had completed his 'Service Militaire' before the war, he returned to his village in the deep tropical forest of Senegal, on the west coast of Africa. Married and with several wives – our sailors and soldiers loved to hear him describe that part of his life, as well as I could translate his deep French patois – there came the day in 1939 when war was declared, and all French reservists were called to the colours. Hundreds of miles away from so-called civilisation, Naboussin heard his army's recall on the jungle drums in his village. We never tired of asking him to imitate those drum calls and with his deep chest he could make our room shake with his amazing mimicry. When the call came he proceeded to walk the many miles to the nearest mobilisation centre.

Of all our preoccupations, food was undoubtedly uppermost in our minds. Or lack of food, should I say – yet again – for I have no sense of embarrassment in recalling those days of hunger. I was over 13 stone when I was captured, and even when I received Red Cross parcels later I was 8 stone, and I was still under 9 stone two years later. But we were lucky. Some of those who went to concentration camps became skeletons.

At Rennes we subsisted on our slices of bread and bowls of soup, for soup is a German speciality, and even in prison it tasted good. Our diet varied with the forces of the market place. If potatoes were in, then potatoes it was, every day, twice a day, until potatoes were no longer available; then cabbages every day, and twice a day, and then cauliflowers. The trouble was that cabbage and cauliflower every day played hell with our insides, and simply tore us to pieces. Happily there were occasional changes of diet, and we had beans, both the large white haricot beans and the little flageolets as they call them in France. They were delicious.

The best meal of all, however, was couscous. None of us had ever tasted it before and it was a luxury prepared by our Arab friends. Couscous can be delicious and, made from semolina, and properly cooked, it is rather like rice. Mixed with lamb it is one of the Arabs' favourite dishes. There wasn't much lamb, but couscous is one of the better memories of those days, and was superior to anything else we had to eat then. Unfortunately, however, it was served only on high days and holidays. Otherwise it was potatoes or cauliflower or cabbage.

Medically, we were cared for as well as the Germans knew how, for with the war in Russia then at its peak, German doctors and nurses were scarce. Fortunately for us, French Army doctors who were prisoners themselves in their own country became responsible for our welfare. Little had they realised that suddenly an additional hundred patients would arrive to join the hundreds of French colonial sick in their care. The senior French medical officer was a Commandant Lacaux – even now more than forty years later I can recall his name without effort. Capitaine Pierre Ryckewaert was next senior: he came from Dunkirk where he had practised before the war. He spoke very good English and was very sympathetic to the British cause. He became our principal interpreter in medical matters. The surgeon who looked after us, Lieutenant Veilleux, on the other hand, was a tough little man from the south of France and violently anti-British. That is not to say that he was pro-German, but he could never forgive the British for destroying the French fleet in 1940 on the north coast of Africa at Mers el Kebir. The other member of the French team was a young medical student, Aspirant Reynaudat, charming and good-looking, who was working to all intents and purposes as a fully qualified doctor despite his lack of qualifications. Such was the shortage of medical practitioners in Europe at that time.

Prisoners themselves and doomed to captivity until the war ended, these French officers nursed us back to health. At first they proceeded to tidy us up as best they could and take over from the Germans' work at La Baule. The transition was fairly painless, and as the days passed our numbers grew fewer, for as soon as someone was able to walk he was literally whisked off to Germany. The reason was not lack of accommodation, there was plenty of that; no, the Germans were fearful of escapers;

and we knew that the French were only too ready to help someone on the run: pilots, aircrews from crashed aircraft, and escaping soldiers. Their courage and help was later to become highly organised and efficient, in spite of the dangers, for if the French, and further north the Belgians and Dutch, were caught helping Allied prisoners in any way, they could expect no mercy from the Germans.

An example of life under the German Occupation happened shortly after we arrived in Rennes. We were still in the small ward, just the officers, for we had been separated from the sailors and soldiers, when one day in the small room we heard someone from next door calling softly to us in English. 'Micky' Wynn, the naval officer, who had lost an eye but who was otherwise on his feet, was waiting for our sentry, in the corridor outside, to walk his beat, and then answered back as best he could. Our windows were barred and this was not easy. It transpired that our neighbour, a French soldier, had escaped from a prison camp in Germany, had returned to his home in Rennes to find his wife. He found her all right, but she was living with a German soldier. She betrayed her husband to the Germans, who arrested him, and brought him to our prison hospital. What happened to him we do not know. He said he was going to be shot – and he had gone the next day. It was an illustration of the uncertainty of life in Europe in those days, and how very dangerous it was to trust anyone – in his case even his wife.

'Micky' Wynn before the war had served as a regular army officer but had been invalided out as unfit. However, he took a small boat to Dunkirk to assist in the evacuation, and afterwards joined the Navy, was commissioned into the RNVR and commanded the fastest vessel at St Nazaire, MTB 74. He wasn't allowed to stay very long at Rennes, because although half blind, he was too active to be trusted. Indomitable and amusing, he still carried his eye with him in the hope that somehow it could be stitched back into the socket. A few days later he left us for Germany, from where he later escaped. (Today he is Lord

Newborough DSC, having succeeded his father.)

Life at Rennes continued, sordid and desperately dull. All hopes of rescue had gone at La Baule, although we had hoped against hope. There seemed nothing to look forward to. But our colonial soldier nurses were in a worse position: they had been prisoners for nearly two years, some of them thousands of miles from their homes and families, yet they could still smile – wonderful smiles – all teeth, and they were genuinely kind and trusting in us. At first it seemed so strange, but on reflection understandable, for we had just arrived in their lives, without warning, aggressors, successful, we had killed a lot of Germans and we had blown up the biggest dry-dock in the world. No wonder they smiled at us.

And so we cheered up and came to look forward to the high points of our lives: food, a nap after luncheon (if one could call it that), and afternoon tea or tisane. The days passed us by and all this time the doctors worked away to help us to recovery.

For me there was little they could do except clean up my arm, and hands, which were full of shrapnel, and which I exercised every night after I received my shot of morphia to dull the pain. I got hooked on morphia, until the doctors stopped dosing me, but it gave me the chance of breaking down the adhesions in my hands. They did nothing to my legs which were still plastered from toes to hips. My legs were also peppered with bits of shrapnel, and to relieve the irritation I made long strips of newspaper which I fed down inside the plaster casts. This helped to assuage the itching. The doctors changed the plaster once, and it was not easy for them to remove a big leg plaster with no bandages separating the plaster of Paris from the hairs on my legs. It was agonisingly painful and later, proper splints were made, with layers of paper bandages next to my skin to keep it from sticking to the actual plaster. Such incidents loomed large in our life at that time.

Others at Rennes were slowly recovering and when able to walk were sent off to German camps. They include such characters as Sub-Lieutenant P.J.C. Dark, RNVR, Lieutenant 'Tiger'

Watson of The Black Watch, Lance-Corporal Arthur Young of the Gordon Highlanders (London Scottish), Lieutenant Etches of the Royal Warwickshire Regiment and No 3 Commando, Lieutenant Gerard Brett, RUR and No 12 Commando, Lance-Sergeant 'Dick' Bradley, Royal Berkshire Regiment and No 2 Commando, and many sailors whose names I regret I cannot remember. By the end of June our numbers had been reduced from over a hundred to fifty and then to no more than about two dozen.

Many months passed. What the doctors were doing was to leave the bullets and shrapnel quiescent in our bodies, and in my case in my knee joints, until the danger of infection had died down to allow them to operate. It was a four-months' wait for me before that took place. The summer brought with it the heat of the sun, and as we lay there sweating, our life became a succession of lazy days. We were now all together in a larger room, officers and men, as we had been before in La Baule. We had received a few books, and the windows were open on to a large playground at the back of the building, which before the war had been a convent school called St Antoine. The French colonial prisoners had installed some form of loudspeaker, from which every day, and all day, droned Arab-type music. After a time we grew to look forward to the call of the midday muezzin and the Arab music which beat out over us all day. What with the heat of the summer, and the lassitude and constant buzzing of flies, life passed us by slowly but surely.

I said we had books. Eventually a limited library of books was sent in to us, from the people of the town outside, and we read and re-read them. I used to be able to remember all the titles but all I can recall now are *Cold Comfort Farm* by Stella Gibbons and *Peking Picnic* by Ann Bridge. The latter was the best escapist story in that limited lending library because, strangely enough, life as described therein *was* escapist.

The food got no better, except that occasionally we received some limited supplies of French Red Cross food. This was nothing on the same scale as we later received from the British Red Cross. At Rennes none of those British supplies came our way, for there in France we were cut off from the main British POW supply lines and no one, other than the Germans, knew where we were. In fact most of us, if not all, were still posted as missing, or missing, believed killed.

There were some isolated incidents which reminded us that there was still a war going on. Daily we heard, and sometimes saw, the Luftwaffe's giant Condor aircraft which used to patrol far out over the Atlantic against Allied shipping. We also used to wake at night to the sound of distant anti-aircraft fire and watch the searchlights sweeping the summer sky for RAF raiders. But we were not on the main stream to anywhere and there were few air raids then.

One day in June there was a lot of shouting and we were locked in our ward. Normally the door was left open, for none of us could walk very well. Naboussin disappeared, and was replaced by a little Negro from Martinique called Joseph. Something was up and we heard eventually, on the grapevine, that more British prisoners had arrived. We could find out no more except that they were sailors and badly wounded.

A few days later they were brought into our room and they told us that they were the survivors of a motor gunboat which had been shot up and sunk in the Channel by German E-boats.

The first time the sailors suspected that there were British soldiers at Rennes was when Naboussin, who had been transferred to look after them, suddenly arrived in their ward, banged his big white hospital jug of tisane on the table and proudly said, 'Ici le fucking tea.' Only British sailors and soldiers could have taught this giant Senegalese to swear in English. He also had another phrase: 'Me black bugger', and other similar terms of endearment. One of our sailors, Able Seaman Albert Sheppard from Nottingham, was his main instructor. Sheppard was only seventeen years old and had had one of his legs amputated below the knee. Naboussin was fond of Sheppard and nursed him like a child, and shook with great laughs as Sheppard taught him English, some of which is unrepeatable, and variations on a theme of blasphemous affection. Whatever he said in his Nottinghamshire dialect, Naboussin just loved it. Naboussin couldn't pronounce Sheppard with the hard 'd' – the best he could muster was 'Shappo'. Funnily enough we never grew so fond of the other nurses as we were of Naboussin. As unofficial interpreter and Senior British Officer (SBO) of the camp, I had a lot of interpreting to do every day and it was said that eventually I spoke with an accent heavily loaded with the patois of Naboussin's Senegalese, and the Arabic of the Algerians and Moroccans.

10

The Professor

In July I was told that I was to be operated on again and one lovely hot day in the early afternoon the nurses came to fetch me on a stretcher. I was taken downstairs and along several corridors to a small dark room and placed on a table. There were two German soldiers armed with rifles – yes, and both wore helmets. One stood on guard at the head of the table and the other at my feet.

A small pleasant-looking man wearing a grey Homburg hat introduced himself as a Professor of Medicine and he proceeded to take off his jacket and start to wash his hands in a wash-basin, all the time smoking dark pungent cigarettes.

A pleasant middle-aged-looking Frenchwoman was also present. She was obviously qualified as a nurse, and she had been seen in Rennes ever since we had arrived there, although she had not been allowed to do much for us except to be friendly in an attempt to show her kind intentions of help. She became a link, although a very small link, with the outside world of wartime France and provincial Brittany. When the Professor had finished 'scrubbing up' he indicated that he was ready to start. As far as I can remember he did not even wear an apron – he certainly wore none of the usual operating theatre overalls and red rubber aprons of the Germans. He was in dark trousers and a waistcoat and still wore his hat. Looking back on that afternoon all I can remember was that there was little real pain, for the kind lady gave me an injection in the base of my spine – a lumbar puncture – which froze the whole of my lower body. I say froze – I could feel no pain – but I was conscious of horrible things happening to me and I sweated pints as the Professor worked away. I could sense roughly what he was doing, and the kind lady sat by me and bathed my head, and whispered sympathetic words in my ear.

The Professor cut and sawed away until I thought he had practically cut my leg off – which he did as far as it was possible in order to get in below the knee-joint and find the bullet lodged there. It was a ricocheting bullet which had hit the road in front of me as I ran with the others towards the Germans desperately trying to stop us. The ricochet stopped me all right; but how did I know it was a ricochet? I saw it flash a yard or so in front of me and the next I knew I was on the ground, stopped. And so the Professor proceeded to clean up my knee and pour sulphur powder into the wound and stitch me up with wire sutures. The wire is still there today.

I said it was hours. I must have dozed off from time to time. At last it was over, but it seemed for ever – I had left my bed at one o'clock and did not get back to the ward until six o'clock.

During the afternoon the Professor smoked incessantly and like all good Frenchmen let his cigarette burn down in his mouth. As the ash grew longer and longer, he then let it drop off from the end of his cigarette on to my leg and sometimes, it seemed, into my wound. But cigarette ash is pure carbon and, as every schoolboy knows, carbon is a good cleansing agent.

One last word about that afternoon: when it was all over and the kind lady gave me a cold rub-down (I was, of course, naked), the Professor patted me kindly on the head and said that it was all over. To which I asked the question: 'Monsieur, will I be able to play rugby again?' To which he bravely said, 'Certainement, mon lieutenant. Rugby and – how do you say, cricket and tennis? – tout va bien – you will soon be on your feet again' – or words to that effect.

Alas, the Professor was being kind and despite his wonderful efforts I never touched a rugby ball again, in play that is. So depressed was I by this that I could never face watching the game played until years later, not even my old club, Wasps, not even international matches.

But I was lucky, for thanks to the French doctors and the

Professor I have my leg still, and so well and quickly did it heal that I was soon trying to escape.

The weather at this time continued to be beautiful and the Germans allowed us to be carried outside and lie in the court-yard, in the sun. But all that happened to me was an attack of severe sunstroke. I suppose I was still too weak and the Germans stopped me sunbathing again.

None of us had tried to escape from Rennes because the Germans posted sentries all around the camp both inside and outside the building. Most alarming, we were on the side of a road, on the other side of which was a large German Head-quarters – if the size of the German flag was any indication – for it was big and red with black cross lines, in the centre of which was the swastika, and we could see German officers and their womenfolk sitting in the garden enjoying the sun.

To escape would be to do so in full view of their windows. In spite of this, however, one of our party, Corporal R. Brown, or 'Nosher' as he was called, a sapper from No 3 Commando, decided one night to make a bid for freedom. We all tried to help by saving pathetic bits of food for him. He was still in his battledress because he was what is still called, with military nicety, 'walking wounded'; and he still had his Commando boots, silent and strong. Night came and for once it was pouring with rain.

No matter, 'Nosher' Brown had declared his intention to me as SBO, and having been given my permission to try, his escape went ahead. For, as so sadly often happened, if there was no organisation* escapers could duplicate each other's efforts or collide in full view of the Germans, with resulting failure and danger to both escapers.

---

* In camps of hundreds and even thousands of prisoners there had to be an efficient control and discipline of those who wished to escape. There were other considerations: food, maps, clothing and money. All major camps were controlled by an Escape Committee with a senior officer or NCO acting as chairman, who, in turn, was answerable to the Germans should anything go wrong.

Brown waited until all was quiet and the internal lights were switched off. Then, as our sentry walked his beat and passed our door to the end of the corridor, Brown slipped out of the room, and crept away in the other direction.

It must have been well after midnight when the door opened and in staggered Brown, dripping wet and shivering with cold. 'What the hell –' we all whispered. 'What happened?' Poor Brown was shaking with cold and it was not until he had stripped off his clothes and got into bed that he made some sense.

He had escaped, but after wandering about the deserted streets he decided it was no good. He obviously was not too strong, he had been in hospital since capture, he was alone, he could not speak a word of French and he had no idea in which direction to go. Furthermore he had no map, and he simply realised that it was 'not on'. Somehow he retraced his steps and climbed back, up, and into the hospital. How he avoided the guards I will never know, except that it was raining so hard no German sentry was going to walk about in that downpour, unless ordered to do so.

Later, when we were transported to Germany, many were the tales of escape or escape attempts, of failure, and of recapture, of utter disaster, and of death even; but with this one amusing exception I never heard of anyone escaping out of prison camp and then climbing back in as did 'Nosher' Brown.

The Germans must have suspected something, or seen his wet footmarks, for we never had another chance like that, and thereafter a sentry stood at our door and kept us under surveillance all the time. Sometimes they showed aggressive tendencies and one day, when we shut the door to have a good look out of the back window for other ways of escape, the next thing we knew the door was literally smashed open and there shouting 'Nein – nein – nein' was a young German soldier shaking with anger and pointing his cocked rifle at us – and his hand was trembling! It was time to freeze again and wait for him to calm down – no wisecracks, no swear words – in those situations silence was golden, and we did not move a muscle.

The men who were with me at Rennes made up my life at that time. There was the young naval sub-lieutenant, Frank Arkle, who grew the most handsome beard of all. We had been given safety razors and very few of us grew beards. There were a number of Petty Officers and seamen of all ranks from *Campbeltown*, most of whom were RN and long-service seamen. The crews of the other vessels, the MTB, the MLs and the MGB, were mostly wartime RNVR officers and ratings. The RN hands had already seen a lot of action by 1942 and were hard men. Their stories of life in the Navy and before the war kept us listening for hours. Whilst not accepting all they said – and they had little respect for army rank – we regarded them as friends.

There was also an intense inter-Service rivalry between the sailors and the Commandos, and our Commando soldiers more than held their own in the eternal day-long arguments. 'Nosher' Brown was particularly adept at baiting the Navy. He had been on the Vaagso raid in 1941, and was a regular soldier, and he was always saying to young Sheppard, the sailor, 'Call yourself a sailor – I've seen more sea-time than you've been in the Navy.'

Sheppard, not to be outdone and despite his extreme youth, would let flow the most awful oaths in reply.

One last memory: although we were completely isolated in a male society, we could see across the courtyard to the back of the hospital. On the other side of the convent wall were houses in which some young girls in their teens lived, presumably with their families. How I will never know, but they got little messages across to us and one sent me her photograph. She was no beauty, but she had a pleasant face and a French charm. In time they sent us chocolate – French chocolate – goodness knows from where they got it. Their feminine presence and kindness, and their messages, became part of our existence. They could not have realised the danger they were in, but like all French people we saw, and those few we were allowed to talk to at La Baule and later at Rennes, they showed their disdain for the occupiers of their beloved France.

I must also place on record our thanks to those French doctors and the nurses at Rennes. Prisoners themselves, they already had enough to do looking after their own sick, of whom there were many, but whatever is the French equivalent to the Hippocratic oath they observed it to the letter, and I for one – and there are others – will always be grateful to them for my health today, more than forty years later.

Of those in the convent hospital at Rennes in 1942 not all survived. Naboussin was reported to have died and never saw the award given to him by King George VI in recognition of his services to us British prisoners. Commandant Lacaux is also reported to have died; he will be remembered for having had to operate on himself in front of a mirror for a hernia while we were there, because he did not trust the Germans. Of the Frenchmen, others were recognised with British awards for helping us, including Capitaine Pierre Ryckewaert and Commandant Lacaux, also Aspirant Reynaudat; and Lieutenant Veilleux who even grew to like us despite his original prejudice against the British.

As we recovered we realised that escape would not be easy, and sure enough in the middle of August we were woken one morning to the usual shouts and told that we were leaving. That is, five of us were leaving, four sailors and myself, leaving Brett, Sheppard, Young and others to stay behind for further treatment.

We five were given a heap of old uniforms, British and French, but not our own, and we were told to get up and get dressed. That sounds easy enough, but it was five months since we had worn anything but old shirts in bed. So we were slow. Eventually I kitted myself out in French army boots, French puttees – blue from the First World War – and some pieces of flannel which they showed us how to wrap round our feet before putting on our boots; for there were no socks and this was our introduction to the 'chaussettes Russes' which the Russians wore. Incidentally, it was then that we learned that the German soldier very rarely wore any socks inside his jackboots. My boots had no surface which would take a shine, but they were very comfortable and rather like the desert boots later made famous by the British Army at El Alamein. For a jacket I found a battledress top, torn and with the black and red pips of the 60th Rifles. I fancied that and therein lies a small tale later. We had no caps or bonnets and just the minimum essential covering; but we made the most of it and tried to look like British Servicemen.

After hasty good-byes, we were taken downstairs to the courtyard and put into a small army truck and there we sat, each with a small haversack containing our worldly belongings, trivial possessions and packs of French cigarettes. We were then exposed to the usual shouting from a German Feldwebel, a sergeant-major, who took several minutes to tell us – if we understood him properly – that if we tried to escape we would be shot. We had been shouted and screamed at for five months already. I had seen one of our soldiers shot as he surrendered, and there were others who were shot as they tried to escape capture. What a stupid joke – did he not realise that we well understood? But he had to go through the pantomime, and he revelled in trying to frighten us. We were not the only ones the Feldwebel used to shout at, as I was to discover, for next day I saw the same form of behaviour, but that was to be in their own country, Germany.

Finally he calmed down, with his soldiers looking on and seemingly rather embarrassed by it all. But one thing we had learned about the Germans: their discipline was rigid and the Feldwebel would just as quickly have turned on *his* soldiers if they as much as showed a wink of sympathy for us.

And so we drove off to Rennes station with our guards, the Feldwebel now quiet, but still jumpy. We were taken on to a long platform crowded with French people and it seemed as if we were to catch a scheduled passenger train with them. The French were not allowed near us and every now and then a guard growled at them to keep their distance. We waited a long time and we had an opportunity of having a first look at wartime Occupied France. France then, as now, had an excitement about it. Its smell then, as now, was quite different, with strong odours of garlic and Gauloise cigarettes. The language even has a vivacity which is strong and vibrant and completely unlike those of the neighbouring countries.

On that wartime day in Rennes, there was no mistaking the fact that, as well as being prisoners of war, we were in France, on the mainland of Europe, and psychologically as far away from home as it was possible to be. The train arrived from Quimper, the Breton town near the coast, with great clouds of steam and the peculiar high-pitched shrieks of a French engine. We climbed up the steep steps into the hard-seated compartment then still in use on continental trains. We did not mind, however, because of the excitement of being on the move again after months of inactivity and boredom. I remember, however, the sense of wariness and suspicion as to where we were going, and what was to be our journey's end. The Germans, somewhat naturally, never told us where we were going.

There was little of interest on that journey except the stop at Laval, an old French town which lies 70 km from Rennes and in the middle of the crossroads of Mayenne, south of Normandy, and on the way to nowhere except Le Mans where the famous 24-hour car race is held; Angers and Tours of historic fame; and Paris, some 300 km to the east. Laval meant nothing to us and it was not until later that I came to appreciate how old a town it was with a history which goes back to the ninth and tenth centuries. We journeyed on for several hours, with several delays. Eventually we began to realise that Paris was our destination. Imagine, Paris, the dream city! I had been to France before the war, but I had never been to Paris. As we rolled through the suburbs we tried to take it all in, although the outskirts of Paris are no more beautiful than those of London. But this was *Paris* and I did not want to miss anything.

The usual black tunnels and approaches to a mainline station, the steam and clatter of the engines, and we rolled slowly

into the Gare Montparnasse. There must have been so much
happening then with our arrival in Paris, getting out of the train
and being herded out of the station, that I have surprisingly
little memory of that first visit to Paris. Later I was to live there,
but even then, as a prisoner, I was attracted by it.

After driving in an army truck across Paris we arrived at the
Gare de l'Est. Here in this much bigger station, crowded with
German soldiers, we parted company, the four sailors on their
way – we did not know it then – to Bremen and the naval camp
Marlag und Milag, and I on my way to Frankfurt-am-Main. As
we stood about waiting for our train, my three guards and
myself, I vaguely thought of escaping. The reaction from
French people everywhere had been one of sympathy, and the
idea grew in my mind that if I could get away, despite my leg,
which was still in bandages and very stiff, I could make it. For,
unlike Brown, I could speak the language reasonably well, and
Paris was a big city. And so I decided to try. First of all I tried
the old trick of asking permission to visit the lavatory. So far, so
good, and I was allowed to go into a cubicle. I locked the door –
but the German guard quite quietly but firmly shouted 'Nein,
nein' so I opened the door with the realisation that my guards
were not that stupid and that was that. I was not depressed, for I
thought that there must be some way of losing the guards, and
of escaping into the helping hands of the French. So I waited for
another chance.

As we waited in the midst of the bustle of the station I
watched my fellow passengers. They were nearly all German
soldiers, and there were officers by the score. They had dozens
of crates of wine which they were loading on to the train
returning them to Germany, presumably on leave. At first I
thought it must be the loot of the conquerors, but later, when I
lived in France and had got to know French people, I realised
that the Germans would have had to pay for it. It was not the
best wine. Years later when I was in Epernay in the famous
cellars of Moët & Chandon, the owner, Comte de Vogué, told
me how they hid the really good wine in the middle of the

millions of bottles of varying ages and quality, none of which is labelled until ready for sale. So how could a stranger, let alone an occupying German soldier, know where the best wine was stored? There are, for example, more than a million bottles of Champagne in any one company's *caves* alone, and there are scores of Champagne companies in Epernay and in Reims, the Champagne region.

Eventually we climbed aboard a train full of soldiers, going home on leave with their wine. I was travelling second-class this time with padded seats and the compartment virtually to ourselves – my three guards and myself – and one other passenger in the light blue uniform of the Luftwaffe. But he kept to himself and said little to the soldiers in charge of me. German discipline and observance of rank was deep-rooted in their system in those days and they, the soldiers, were there only because I was there. Prisoner though I was, I seemingly warranted comfortable accommodation on this train. It was a form of compliment to be so well guarded, but I did not appreciate such protection and comfort – I wanted to get away.

The train suddenly started, only to stop a few minutes later, with the usual rattle and steam of those days. I decided to try again, and I asked permission to go to the lavatory once more. The guards swore, although quietly, but after a bit of an argument, one of them stood up and, taking his rifle, ushered me out into the corridor and to the lavatory at the end of the carriage. He let me in to the small space and pulled the door to. I waited for a moment or so then quietly opened the small window and poked my head out into the night air to find myself looking down a railway embankment falling away into the dark. At the foot of the embankment were some houses and I could make out chinks of light through blackout curtains. I looked to my left, towards the front of the train, and then to my right. There, cheerfully and quietly, stood my guard, looking at me from the window of the carriage door. Obviously he was no fool and that was that, for he seemed to know all the answers. Reluctantly I backed into my small lavatory prison, opened the door and let myself be pushed quite gently along the corridor to my compartment. The train was soon on the move again and very quickly was roaring through the night towards the east.

Back in the compartment I tired of thoughts of escape, and soon fell asleep. A mistake, yes, but I was very very tired, and this was my first day out of hospital after lying in bed for five months. Every time the train slowed or stopped I woke to find one of the soldiers awake and looking at me, and I dozed back into resignation. Not despair – I had long since conquered that emotion. Resignation, yes, but only as a temporary expedient. Tomorrow was another day.

It must have been very early in the morning – it was still dark – as we slowed and came to rest in another large station, Metz, near the frontier between France and Germany. We stopped there for a long time. Strange as it may seem, then in Occupied Europe, a Europe united by force, the normal Customs and frontier checks were still being observed.

While we waited, the guards took turns to visit the soup kitchen on the platform and get their rations. Each one was given a large bowl of soup and an enormous slice of black bread and margarine. As one of the party I was allowed to take my turn. When I say soup, there were no words to describe those German soup kitchen soups. They were very filling, mostly potatoes, with meat even, and were served to all soldier passengers on German trains. It was the first time that I had tasted, let alone eaten, such a luxury in my five months of captivity. In the months to come whenever I was on a train journey – alas, it was not often – I always looked forward to those soldier soup kitchens for the soup was incomparably better than the thin liquid soups served to us in our prison camps. Therein was a widely differing interpretation of the rules as contained in the Geneva Convention. To be unkind, but fair, German prisoners in Britain, and later across the Atlantic, were fed like our own troops, as the Convention specified. But the Convention did not work reciprocally with prisoners in Germany excepting, as I have said, when we were in small groups, or alone, and being transported in a train from camp to camp.

Having eaten we climbed back into the train. I was exhausted and in no mood to upset my guards, so I slept or dozed through the night. Dawn broke and I had my first look at Germany. I was depressed and felt lost. My pathetic attempts to escape had been of no avail. The further we travelled into Germany the further I would have to walk out of Germany, if, and I say if, I could get away. As the train rolled on, we passed through forests of trees and then into a very large city. It was Frankfurt-am-Main, one of the largest cities in Germany, and it was already awake.

By this time it was about half past seven in the morning, and when our train stopped in the station, we found ourselves in the middle of the German morning rush hour. At least that is what it seemed to me; everywhere I looked I saw men and women hurrying on their way with the characteristic German satchel or briefcase under their arm. Even the German soldiers carried a briefcase. Once again we stood about on a railway platform – we had moved from one platform to another – and one of my guards went off to get fresh instructions. There were many people there, many more than I had seen in Paris, but not so many soldiers.

Suddenly, and with shouts, a column of grey-coloured figures advanced, or rather stumbled towards us. They were surrounded by soldiers, only soldiers with a difference. They were, as I was to find out later, members of the dreaded Sicherdienst-Polizei. Their uniforms were greener than that worn by the Wehrmacht – a 'bright' green. They had steel helmets, jackboots, and large shining breastplates hanging from chains around their necks – breastplates shaped like large kidney beans. They were second only to the SS in brutality and they burst into my view pushing and herding a column of figures – the figures of women – along in front of them, stuffing their rifle butts into and up them, as the wretched creatures stumbled past us, so close that they brushed against my clothes.

The women all wore head shawls, and they did not look like the German women on the station. I could only guess that they were from Eastern Europe, maybe Russia, for later in Germany I was to see hundreds, thousands even, of women prisoners like them. As they disappeared down the long platform I had an immediate sense of shock, horror even, for I had never seen anything so brutal as that dreadful treatment of those women. One of the women, in the middle of the group, had stopped to pick up a cigarette end, right in front of me, about a foot away, no more, and as she did so she received the full force of a German's rifle up her backside. She screamed but somehow kept her feet and staggered on.

I suddenly realised that this really was Nazi Germany. And I am sorry to say that the many German civilians waiting there for their trains on that early summer morning in 1942 were witnesses of the scene. They did nothing, they could do nothing. With the episode still troubling me I left Frankfurt on another, slower train. I tried to remember where we were going but all I could recall of that day was miles and miles of forest and pretty German towns.

We were in fact travelling due north through Westphalia, a few kilometres from where the Iron Curtain now divides Germany.

I do not even remember arriving at our destination except that it was a small station and that there was the inevitable army truck waiting for us. We were at a place called Spangenberg. Spangenberg is a very old town, and was later partially destroyed by the Americans in the fighting in 1945. I remember being in a lovely old house, requisitioned by the army, and then used as some sort of Military Headquarters. There I met a strange man, well educated, wearing a wooden leg, an officer from the First World War, a Hauptmann in the German army; a man who was indirectly to influence my life as a prisoner for the next year and a half.

He was Hauptmann Heyl, one of a group of security officers controlling the complex of POW camps at Spangenberg, better

known as the 'top camp' and the 'bottom camp' – so called
because one was at the top and one at the bottom of a small but
steep hill. I did not know it then but I was in the Kommandantur of the two camps. There I was questioned again, but it
was nothing more than a formality, and they got nothing other
than rank, name and number. I had anyway been a prisoner for
nearly six months and my information, if any, was by then out
of date. After the questions and a show of activity by the
Germans, I was escorted out of the building through the back
streets of a lovely old town and out into the surrounding
countryside. The buildings of the village were all built of faded
red, almost pink, coloured brick – half-timbered and distinctly
bucolic in appearance. The whole scene, brief though it was,
was pervaded with a sleepy warm atmosphere and a pungent
smell of dung; a country smell which was not unpleasant and
not unlike the smell of France where I had just come from – but
much stronger.

As we walked along a tree-lined lane with a broken cobbled
surface, I was slow – I had only been out of bed for two days and
the going was difficult. Very shortly the road rose in front of us
up a quite steep hill. It twisted and turned with the contours
and, suddenly, looming up out of the trees, was a castle with
turrets and small windows – a real *Schloss*. As we approached it
there in front of us was a large moat and a bridge which spanned
a gap of about 20 ft. On our side of the bridge was a sentry-box
painted in red and black diagonal stripes – the pattern of army
sentry boxes wherever we went in Germany. I never did discover the reason for that colour scheme.

11

Spangenberg Castle

Pushing me gently, and without any further ceremony, one of my guards indicated that I had to cross the bridge. There, on the other side, waiting for me was a surprising sight: after months of French hospitals was a white-haired, distinguished-looking man in khaki service dress, breeches and puttees and red tabs, and the shoulder badges of a major-general in the British Army. As I limped towards him he held out his hand and said, 'I can't really welcome you here, but it's good to see you. My name is Fortune.' And looking at my red pips said, 'I see you're in the 60th' [the 60th Rifles – now the Green Jackets].

I stopped and, coming to attention in front of him, said: 'Sir, thank you, but I'm not in the 60th, I'm a Gordon Highlander.' 'Never mind,' he said, 'come in and meet everyone.' I have never forgotten that scene and the mixed emotions I had at meeting General Victor Fortune, then the Senior British Officer of all British prisoners in Europe at that time – some 200,000 officers and men. The General had served with great distinction when commanding the 51st Highland Division in 1940 and went into captivity with his Scottish troops after fighting a valiant rearguard at St Valéry, to the south of Dunkirk.

But I did not have a second to myself, for immediately I was surrounded by other prisoners, and friends of mine who had been captured at St Nazaire, some of whom had been in hospital with me in La Baule and Rennes.

There was our Colonel, Charles Newman, later to be awarded the VC, still beaming with his cheerful smile and sucking his pipe; Major Bill Copeland; there was 'Micky' Burn of the 60th, whose jacket it was that I was wearing; Ronnie Swayne, with whom I had dined, both in Cardiff in reality and in my nightmare at La Baule. There were about fifteen or sixteen of them, the only survivors of the original thirty-nine Commando officers who had been on the St Nazaire raid.

There were also about 200 other officers from nearly every regiment in the British Army. They had been prisoners since the fighting in 1940, and a few who had been caught in Greece, and Crete, and in the early fighting in North Africa. They were as curious to see me as I was to see them and, as I was one of the St Nazaire party, they accepted me quickly and without suspicion, except for my 60th jacket; there were several officers from that regiment in the camp, but they were soon reassured. I use the word 'suspicion' because suspicion governed life in prison and, as the war ground on, the hundreds of thousands of prisoners of all ranks and nationalities increased as battle succeeded battle, and it was difficult to check identities and the stories of those who said they were on our side. We tried to guard against suspicion, but not always successfully, and this was to have tragic consequences for us later.

The castle on the top of the hill was basically several hundred years old and had been used earlier as a prison camp in the Napoleonic wars. It was virtually escape-proof. Although re-built and modernised before our war the layout of the castle, probably originally medieval, was patterned on the ancient concept of a huge outer wall which formed a rough elongated square the inside of which was a courtyard, cobbled and large enough to form an area about 100 ft long and 50 ft wide. We were allowed to move about freely during the day. Twice a day the courtyard and precincts of the castle, including the moat, served as a parade ground where we were counted in the morning and again in the evening. During night-time we were locked in the rooms all round the castle with the intention of preventing movement by us between rooms until next day. At least that was the intention, but movement between 200* restless prisoners

---

* Oflag IX AH ('top camp') at that time had 190 senior officers and 36 British POW orderlies. The 'bottom camp' in the village of Spangenberg had 216 officers and 34 British POW orderlies (Public Record Office Reports).

was virtually impossible to prevent however vigilant the guards were.

That first night was a blur of excitement and greetings, but I was grateful when I was shepherded into the small camp hospital high up in a turret of the castle. There I slept, albeit fitfully, through the night, conscious only of being in a completely different atmosphere from that of Rennes.

Although Spangenberg, Oflag IX AH, was a small camp, there was a feeling of restlessness quite unlike the comparative quiet of hospital life in France. Here were men who had been captured intact and whose frustration was paramount. Here the guards were more alert and, when I woke during the night, I could hear the barking of dogs – big dogs by the sound of them – and when the guards were changing sentry, their words of command were incisive and had a ring of aggression more marked in their intonation than their predecessors' in Rennes.

When I woke that first morning it was bright daylight with sounds of movement all over the place. That first morning, too, I was 'counted' lying fully dressed on my cot while the roll-call ('Appel') took its course.

So far I have described nothing but a disjointed sequence of incidents which occurred with no fixed pattern or continuity. But at Spangenberg life began to take on a more even course at last – tedious for the most part, but with its highlights of excitement and humour.

'Appels' dominated our lives and forcibly reminded us that there we were locked up, hundreds of miles from home – thousands of miles for the Australians, New Zealanders and Indians. There were, as I have said, hundreds of thousands of us, millions even, all prisoners, if we counted the Poles, French, Dutch and the Russians – surely the largest concentration of men in captivity that had ever been known in history. And 'Appels' like ours took place all over Europe every morning, and every evening, as the Germans counted us and recounted to see that no one was missing. Naturally people went missing; when that happened 'Appels' were called again and again until

the Germans' love of order was restored, or they had to accept that an escape had broken through their security.

A typical 'Appel' was preceded by loud shouts of 'Aus – aus' and then a variation of 'schnell, schnell, aus, alles aus' as our guards stomped through the buildings of each particular camp ordering everyone out on to the parade grounds. There we were slowly organised into squads of a hundred or more, in rows of five.

In Spangenberg we were arranged in three squads forming a hollow square. When, as then, the weather was fine, we took our time and stretched the guards' patience as far as we thought suitable on the day in question. The only exception was when it rained, or later, during the winter, when it was snowing in sub-zero temperatures; so cold that we used to get frost-bitten. The great point of daily 'Appels' was that it provided the only formal way of showing our resistance to captivity; and 'Appel' became a battle of wits between those who had guns and the authority of power, and those of us who had nothing but the nerve and will to resist. When 'Appel' was finished, and the Senior British Officer had saluted the senior German officer, we were dismissed and became free once more to follow our own devices.

But first of all came breakfast, if it could be called that. Basically it was always the same food: acorn coffee and black bread – but now there was a difference – British Red Cross parcels.

To those who have never lived near to or at starvation level, it is difficult to explain what that difference was like. The Red Cross have always been highly organised and courageous, as witness the stories of the First World War hospitals and their nurses. The Red Cross has also long been the symbol of mercy and sacrifice. It has inspired numerous writers, for example Ernest Hemingway and his ambulance drivers at Caporetto. But there can be nothing to compare with the life-saving results of the Red Cross parcels received by prisoners in those years of captivity in the Second World War.

Each parcel weighed 20 lb and contained one tin each of margarine, meat, sardines, jam and condensed milk. There was a ¼ lb bar of chocolate, orange juice crystals, some biscuits, a tin of Bemax cereal. We received a parcel each, one a week, the same for each prisoner, no matter what rank or service; for there was no division of class in a prison camp. There were exceptions for the seriously wounded – by that I mean those who lived in camp hospitals, or who were ill with cancer or TB; they received the so-called 'invalid parcels' which contained slightly more of the same ingredients as in the ordinary parcels with the emphasis on butter and other life-saving foods, unobtainable even in war-time Britain. When Americans were taken prisoner the next year in North Africa, or were shot down in air raids on Germany, they received a slightly different type of parcel with some wonderful variations on our parcels. That does not mean to say that we ever complained of such comparisons. Whenever, later, we were to be with American and Canadian prisoners they generously shared their marginally better food with us; and when the odd Polish and Czech pilots, and servicemen from other countries, including Indians from the battlefields of North Africa and Italy, arrived at the camp, they were immediately put on the Red Cross ration strength for food parcels, although some of the food was unacceptable to their religious beliefs.

Anyway, on that first morning in Spangenberg, there I was spreading margarine, real margarine, on my slice of bread, and then, luxury of luxuries, covering that with a thin scraping of jam. I say thin, because even those parcels would not allow for extravagance if they were to last through a week.

What would we have done without those parcels? I often thought back to Rennes, where we were off the beaten track of the Red Cross supply lines, and we had no life-giving delicacies such as they then provided.

Breakfast over I was shown around the confines of the castle. Everywhere there were prisoners. The place was like an ant-hill. Reading seemed to be the main order of the day, and every

conceivable nook and cranny of the old building was occupied by reclining figures, some alone.

The sun was shining in a clear blue sky, the prisoners' dress varied from nothing but shorts, faded and torn, to a more formal dress of trousers, open-neck shirt and neck scarf. In fact some were smart and rather dressy; others, the complete reverse, dirty even, in their torn clothing.

There were others, playing strange games adapted to the close limits of the courtyard. Every now and then a German would enter the camp yard, through the only gate, invariably escorting an officer prisoner, engaged on some household chore. For a community of 200, all living in a small confined space, was bound to create household problems: lavatories and kitchens, disease and smell, to name but a few. In every camp that I ever lived in there was an uneasy truce between captive and captor, but to try and control such household chores was a problem that needed constant attention. Months later we were made brutally conscious of this problem of togetherness: for if we the prisoners were in danger of infection, so were our guards.

At that time the war in Russia was at its most intensive. Millions on both sides were involved and the fighting was desperate – and so was the threat of disease. No one was immune. The word typhus strikes a note of fear in the hearts of even the uneducated. Fleck typhus is worst, and if fleck typhus had swept into Europe from the East, D-Day would probably not have been necessary. And so when typhus started to gain control in Russia and Poland, the Germans realised that with millions of prisoners in their midst they had a virtually uncontrollable problem, which no preventive medicine then available could control.

Months later every prisoner was inoculated by the Germans against typhus; and we were inoculated, each one of us, as we stood on parade, with a blunt needle which they stuck into the rib-cages of our chests – such was their fear of that dreaded plague.

So there we were; locked up in a rather gloomy castle in Spangenberg, situated in the province of Hesse-Nassau near Kassel, the former capital of Hesse. The castle was for British officers of field rank and up, plus a few junior officers, including ourselves. We subalterns were a bit out of place there, but such was the Germans' concern as to what we had done at St Nazaire, and their fear of our potential as escapers – some had got away already – that we were locked up in this castle. Colditz, a much more famous prisoner-of-war castle, where some of our party were eventually sent, was not as difficult as Spangenberg to escape from and to my own knowledge no one ever escaped and reached home from the 'top camp' at Spangenberg during those years.*

Apart from the small hospital in one of the turrets the rest of the prisoners were crowded into small rooms hanging, as it were, from the very turrets of the castle and connected one to the other by steep winding staircases. After a few days in the hospital I was moved down into the largest room in the castle, where the junior officers were congregated. There were some twenty of them squeezed into this room; those from St Nazaire, and a few others who had drifted into Spangenberg during their months of captivity mostly by some quirk of fate and particularly when recaptured after escaping. The room was noisy and we were all young. It was mostly bedlam and was dubbed the 'Arab quarter'. That was not meant as disrespect, rather was it indicative of constant noise, movement, and the expression of youth; for the rest of the camp was full of older men who although brave and wise were, some of them, sadly resigned to despair.

I soon became integrated into life in the 'top camp' and became

* But others, including Airey Neave and our own Billy Stevens, were among others who did escape from Colditz.

just another prisoner, because that is all I was. One thing became immediately apparent, however, and that was that after five months in hospital I had become slow in my reactions and slow to understand quite what was happening. This was forcibly brought home to me by one of my fellow officers, Corran Purdon, who snapped at me for being so slow on the uptake. He was right, but then he had not been in hospital for several months. Later, when I regained my wits, and with some measure of mental ability to answer back, I realised how much one loses, lying in bed and listening to a day-long monologue of limited conversation, with no books and no mental stimulation.

It is difficult to describe prison life without referring to escape. As in other prison camps, escape at Spangenberg was a priority, and very quickly I realised that much nefarious activity was going on. Although there were those who secretly had given up any idea of life other than captivity, there was an active and aggressive element of those who wanted to implement the British Army's standing order, that all prisoners-of-war should do their utmost to escape. There were others who also saw in that order a means of defiance, and some there were who met their death more in defiance rather than in attempting to escape.

The first escape effort quickly became apparent to me when, a few mornings after arrival, I was witness to a strange event that occurred with increasing frequency in the days to follow. This consisted of the removal of footrests from the long desks in the castle, taken into the courtyard, where they were bolted together and restructured into the form of a crane, the length of which was intended to span the moat. I say 'crane' for it was designed to swing out and over the moat and then rest on the parapet on the other side; whereupon the would-be escapers standing in the moat below would climb up a rope-ladder connected to the end of the crane and thus escape into the trees.

There were other schemes: one consisted of digging down through the floor of the castle into solid rock – sufficiently far down, that is, to dig out a sap into the hillside and into the trees and away. All right in principle, but digging down through solid rock with makeshift home-made tools takes time. Another, more obvious, scheme was somehow to walk out of the front gate. That was not as impossible as it sounds, for similar efforts to walk out of the front gate of other camps had succeeded.

I was only an observer at that time, because it would have been an imposition to break into a 'scheme'. It seemed to me that the situation was no better than at Rennes. It all seemed rather amateurish, but then maybe I was jaundiced with what I saw.

No matter – it was evident that there was a continuing effort to escape, and it kept the Germans on the hop, as shown by their nervous reactions and alarms. We, on our part, were ever optimistic and my brother officers were unceasing in their work to find some way of leaving captivity. In the book *MI9: Escape or Evasion 1939-45* M.R.D. Foot and J.M. Langley describe the various camps in Germany and mention how Spangenberg presented almost insuperable difficulties.*

I will not attempt to chronicle all that went on in that camp; life there was little different from life in the camp below – the 'bottom camp' Oflag IXA (or Haine Kloster as it was known) – where Foot and Langley describe how 200 officers were crowded into a space only 75 yds square surrounded by a barbed wire fence 9 ft high and 9 ft thick. Although the two camps were less than 1 km apart, and we had the same guards and Kommandantur, the separation was absolute. Of the would-be escapers, the leaders included our Robert Montgomery, who indeed had helped to build the crane device from the dining-room table.

There was another St Nazaire survivor – a small bespectacled figure in the Intelligence Corps, Antony Imbert-Terry†,

* Corran Purdon and 'Dickie' R.F. Morgan, another St Nazaire officer, did get out of Spangenberg, but were recaptured and sent to Colditz.
†Imbert-Terry was later, and for several years, the correspondent for the *Sunday Times* in Germany.

who was with us on the raid to help as interrogator of German prisoners. Sadly for him there was little interrogating for him to do. Here at Spangenberg he was trying a 'front gate' scheme – something to do with the horse and cart which every day was dragged up the hill and into the castle with our rations, and then left again with our rubbish and potato peelings from our staple diet. Terry was to be hidden in the cart before it departed down the hill, or was to hide under the cart – but he never made it while I was there.

For those who had little interest in escape there was a small library, musical instruments, and all the time in the world. There were daily lectures on every conceivable subject. To name just some: there was an enthusiastic 'sailing club' where prisoners literally learnt to sail a boat on a blackboard instructed by a stocky little major who had been a yachtsman before the war. There were seminars, accompanied by our gramophone, on music of every kind. There were even lessons in the German language (not very popular); lessons in lock-picking to aid would-be escapers, and religious instruction for those who felt the need – as many of us did.

A number of prisoners were cavalry officers, and at Spangenberg and other camps, the plans for the post-war British Equestrian Team, later to win gold medals in the Olympic Games and at international events all over the world, were made by Colonel 'Mike' Ansell, who had been blinded, Colonel Harry Llewellyn, of 'Fox-hunter' fame, and Jack Fawcus, a pre-war Grand National rider.

And there were those who, with great determination and concentration, sat down and studied for university degrees and to qualify as doctors and lawyers.

As in most camps there was an active theatre group, and an enthusiastic and competent camp orchestra. As new arrivals we were asked to put on a show for the camp. Written by 'Micky' Burn, who was a *Times* correspondent before the war, and assisted by Gerard Brett, an archaeologist and curator of the Victoria and Albert Museum, it was a musical skit on the life of prisoners-of-war, 'ancient Brits' and slaves in ancient Rome. The show was a success and was enjoyed by our older fellow prisoners. Like all POW shows it was full of sly digs at our captors, but the German officers – who were always given the best seats – seemed to enjoy themselves. If there was offence they did not show it. I don't remember the plot – if there was one – but I clearly recall our costumes, coarse white hospital sheets wrapped round our middles, with nothing else except our heavy Commando boots. I was lent a pair – and our only other costumes were 'dog tags', our identity discs. The music was modern and noisy.

Like everything in prison, there was the inevitable reaction after the show, a feeling of let-down and depression. But it had been fun. Later productions were more ambitious and included *The Devil's Disciple* and *The Man of Destiny* by Shaw. Here was real theatre and drama, and emotional scenes during production not far different from those I was to see after the war with Noël Coward, David Lean, Ann Todd and others when I worked in Pinewood Studios.

It was after our first camp show at Spangenberg that frustration boiled over one afternoon, in the form of a quite dangerous battle fought between the inmates of the 'Arab quarter'. We fought each other to a standstill – our weapons were our metal washbasins which, when spun through the air, could do quite serious harm to those who were not quick enough to duck. It was a scene reminiscent of our schooldays, and no quarter was given. Despite the cuts and bruises, no one was seriously hurt; it cleared the air and we enjoyed letting off steam. Our senior officers were not impressed and put it down to lack of discipline.

12

I Leave Spangenberg, Alone

My stay in Spangenberg was short. Two or three weeks after I crossed the castle moat, I had to leave the camp and my friends. There was no warning of departure from the camp – there never was, principally because of the oft-repeated attempts in the early days of captivity to exchange identities between the intended traveller and a would-be escaper.

Again, with a quota of three guards, I was put on a train to go to another hospital. Our journey was short but seemed to take a long time. We went east towards Leipzig following the River Fulda, a slow-running stream which meanders through lovely country and tree-topped hills on both sides, rather like the upper reaches of the Thames at Goring and Streatley. After a few miles we arrived at Eisenach not far from Leipzig. There we changed trains. As we waited, my guards were asked by my fellow travellers, soldiers of all ranks, what I was doing there. Their curiosity was friendly, and even tinged with the respect that one soldier has for another. And they always showed respect for the wounded.

In addition to the army soldiers, there were some SS troops in their sinister black uniforms with skull-and-crossbones badges on their caps – fore-and-aft hats we called them in the British Army. There were also some extremely smart and seasoned-looking troops in green, with ankle-length puttees, wearing narrow peaked caps. I found out later that they were 'Jaeger' or mountain troops. They were all travelling east and I could only assume they were returning to the Russian front, or the 'Ost-front', as they called it, from leave.

It was then late summer of 1942 and the dreadful winter fighting of 1941 and 1942 had taken its toll of the German army, but there was no sign of defeat in the eyes of these men. On the contrary – they were full of confidence and arrogance.

On the journey to Eisenach the train had been packed with civilians and we had to stand. After some time the passengers relaxed; they started talking to my guards and asked who I was. As the guards replied, and almost proudly said, 'Ein Engländer – ein offizier', they all looked at me with increased interest and curiosity. Suddenly a middle-aged woman stood up and offered me her seat, saying to the guards, 'Er ist ein offizier und verwundet' – and she insisted that I sit down. I often wondered if such treatment would have been forthcoming for a German POW officer in a carriage full of civilians in wartime Britain. I doubt it. Anyway I was grateful, and tried to express my thanks, and then fell asleep. When I woke again, she had gone, and with her a gesture from a kind little woman in wartime Germany.

We arrived at another POW hospital, small and full of wounded from other theatres of war including North Africa. It was called Ober Masfeld.

I was never told why I was sent to Ober Masfeld. I can only assume that the Spangenberg doctor, Jimmy James, was worried about my knee, and the post-operational effects of the French Professor's work in Rennes. There were many other orthopaedic cases at Ober Masfeld and the Senior British Officer was the leading orthopaedic surgeon and specialist, Bill Tucker, then a colonel.

Bill had been captured at the time of Dunkirk and was now in charge of this hospital with several limbless and lame cases such as myself. Bill – a large man – had played rugby for Cambridge University and several times for England in the 1930s, and after the war became well known looking after footballers and other athletes. But at Ober Masfeld he had a different role and he performed it well. He has enormous hands, but surprisingly for a forward he used them then with great skill and unusual deftness. However, he could find little wrong with the Professor's work and there was nothing more that he and his fellow doctors could do for me so I was allowed to lie there in his hospital for the next few days, until he received further movement orders for me.

It was September 1942 when a trainload of recently wounded prisoners arrived. They had been caught during the Canadian Army and British Commando raid in Dieppe the month before. They must have been travelling across Germany for weeks before they arrived at our camp. I was allowed to visit them in their part of the hospital. As I entered their ward – it was early autumn and hot – the stench was overpowering, so much so that I could not stand it for long. I had to leave the ward for the open courtyard of the camp literally gasping for breath.

It was only then that I realised what I must have smelled like a few months before, and what the others must have smelled like in our stuffy hospital in Rennes. It brought back the memory of Sheppard's horror when the doctors wiped his stump clean after Veilleux cut away his bandages weeks after we had been captured, for there on the stump of his amputated leg were maggots which, horrific though they seemed, had cleaned his wound and helped the healing processes of the human body. One clean swab, and there was the shining pink skin of a healed wound, with no infection. When the doctors opened the 'windows' on the plaster casts of my legs to examine the bullet and shrapnel holes for signs of infection they unleashed a smell which must have been the same as the stench from those fellow Canadian prisoners at Ober Masfeld.

At Ober Masfeld I remember lying on a comfortable bed in a hospital ward; Red Cross parcels; and lazy hours of idle talk during those hot autumnal days, getting to know each other. As we lay there the soldiers took turns to amuse us, but the prisoner whom I particularly remember was a fellow Commando officer, caught and seriously wounded during the raid on Rommel's HQ in the desert. He was Robin Campbell*, a captain, who was

* Campbell was another ex-journalist, with Reuters, son of the British Ambassador in Portugal, Sir Ronald Campbell – known as 'Big Ronnie' compared to the other 'Ronnie', then our First Secretary in Washington and later Sir Ronald Campbell, our Ambassador in Cairo, uncle of another fellow prisoner, David Campbell.

handsome but at that time cynical and sour in his outlook. When one soldier, holding the stage in our ward, repeated the ditty: 'Poor Miss Ormsby-Gore/She was not very rich and she was not very poor', followed by some rather questionable observations, Campbell said suddenly: 'Do you realise that you are talking about my wife?'

Almost immediately I was on the move again, on a train, but going back westwards. I remember that I was soon back in Eisenach changing trains once more. As we stood about in an informal group in the autumnal sun with our guards, I saw for the first time, face to face, the tough, fierce faces of some Russians. They were dressed in surprisingly bright green uniforms, brighter in colour than any German uniforms I had seen so far. They wore breeches but had no puttees, and they had crude-looking shoes. They had forage caps, but no regimental signs or badges of rank. A few German guards were with them but they were not nearly so closely guarded as we were. Our guards shouted at them to keep clear as they cried 'cigarette, cigarette' – the universal currency of all prisoners then. As we thrust a handful of cigarettes towards them, two or three of them nearest to us snatched them out of our hands, nearly tearing our fingers off, and just as quickly stuffed the cigarettes into their mouths. Our guards shouted at them to keep clear and pushed them away.

I have often wondered what those ragged and starving Russians did with those few cigarettes. Did they hide them in their mouths until they could be removed, dried out and smoked later out of sight of the Germans? Or were they chewed into quids, then rolled in their mouths to savour the tobacco juice? If they did I suspect they would have swallowed the juices, for there were no cuspidors in prisoner-of-war trains in wartime Germany.

I will never forget the ferocity of those soldiers, and I was later to see more of them – thousands of them – working on the land near our camp. In fact there were millions of them all over Germany at that time, working in factories and coalmines.

Without their labour it is possible that the war would have been drastically shortened.

We waited for our train, and our guards calmed down. Suddenly another startling scene unfolded before us. A train slowly rolled alongside the platform on which we were waiting, a long goods train made up of wagons with the doors bolted shut. Very slowly it came to a stop with the usual clanking and clattering noise of railway trucks being shunted together. As we looked at the wagons we heard voices, then to our horror we could see human eyes looking through the cracks of the doors and through the gaps between the slats of the truck sides – then more eyes at all levels and the tips of human fingers.

We realised that the train was packed with human bodies – alive and mumbling some foreign language we could not recognise. After the cigarette incident our guards were much too alert to allow us to try anything, and all we could do was to stand helplessly there and, without a word from us or the Russians or the Germans standing nearby, the train slowly started to move again, and was very slowly shunted out of the station, clanking and rattling with the peculiar continental shriek of the engine's whistle and noise of a heavy train moving east.

By this time we were comparatively hardened to scenes of horror, and I doubt if we realised then the enormity of what we had just witnessed, for the terrible story of concentration camps – if that is where the prisoners were being taken – was only just emerging to us in all its horror.

There were many similar scenes from those days in Europe, and when some people express disbelief of wartime barbarity, and sub-human cruelty, they only express their ignorance or their selfishness in not wishing to know, or fear of being accused of complicity in those wartime crimes in Nazi Germany.

I do not believe we even appreciated the fact that these people in the train were probably of German origin. Their language did not sound like German, but none of us in our small group could understand German then. They could have been Dutch or

Flemish – they certainly were not French or I would have understood some of their pleadings.

But before we could think more about that train going east, our own train arrived, going west. It was made up of old carriages and goods trucks and we were pushed into one of the trucks. This was the first time that I was to travel in a goods truck. The Germans had opened the big sliding doors wide, so that we could sit on the floor of the truck and swing our legs out over the side – not very comfortable, but the weather was fine and it gave us a feeling of comparative freedom. Later we came to realise that the whole of the German Army was moved about in this way, just as they had been in the previous war, and it is perhaps best illustrated by the French, who did likewise and who then still had stencilled on the side of their rolling-stock '40 hommes et 8 chevaux'.

Once again we were rolling along by the Fulda through the same lovely wooded country, but this time in the same direction as the river's current. I thought we were returning to Spangenberg, but I was to be disappointed. As always in prison life the move proved just one more frustration, an example of our helplessness in the grip of German officialdom. Although we were in the same military region of Germany, the IX Military Region, we were on our way to Rotenburg-am-Fulda, to another camp called Oflag IX AZ, a few miles from Oflag IX AH, the castle on the hill.

13

Rotenburg-am-Fulda

Oflag IX AZ was right on the banks of the River Fulda – a large, relatively modern building cocooned in more barbed wire than anywhere I had seen so far. Before the war it had been a large school for girls and was alleged to have been the background for the celebrated film *Mädchen in Uniform* (1931).

Rotenburg was nothing special to look at, but in appearance it was deceptively easy for a would-be-escaper. It was five storeys tall with a very high attic roof. But it had few of the outhouses and other adjacent buildings so attractive to an escaper, who was always looking for shadows and cover, from wall to wall, to help him get away. Sitting flat on the meadows of the River Fulda it was a formidable camp, as we later found out. It was called the 'Jakob Grimm Schule', and grim it was.

We prisoners occupied most of the main building but one end was blocked off with barbed wire. It formed the German Kommandantur and quarters for the German sentries. Rotenburg was much larger than Spangenberg, containing 353 officers, mostly British. Later, in April 1943, the camp had to accommodate 566 prisoners-of-war of all nations, again mostly British, but including 154 American officers. Foot and Langley describe how these included an 'unusually large number of elderly officers', which is perhaps why, according to some Dominion prisoners, the camp was over-organised from an escape point of view; despite its deceptively easy appearance, only two officers ever got away from there.

Rotenburg also contained 79 other ranks employed to look after the officers, for the camp held a comparatively large proportion of disabled and blind officers who had been collected together in the event of repatriation being agreed between the two warring powers. Repatriation under the terms of the then current Geneva Convention, signed on 6 July 1906, meant that officers and men who had been wounded, and were in captivity, would be exchanged as soon as possible. That was the intention, but the Germans had other plans.

As events in Czechoslovakia and Poland had shown, such conventions only meant anything to the Germans when it suited them; so that whilst in 1942 there were several thousand Allied prisoners who should have been repatriated under the conditions of the Geneva Convention, there had been no major Allied victories in early 1942 and the British had only captured a few hundred Germans, mostly pilots and seamen. In the case of Japan the situation was even more critical, for although there were hundreds of thousands of British, Commonwealth and American prisoners in Japanese POW camps, the Japanese did not recognise the Geneva Convention. They did not even recognise the fact that a soldier could be captured; rather, he should die as his rightful duty. Likewise the Russians did not admit to Geneva, nor to the Red Cross.

There had been exchanges of prisoners between Britain, France and Germany in the First World War and the Germans had then exercised a degree of humanity in allowing repatriation of padres and of doctors who had stayed with their wounded in the face of threatened and ultimate capture. But the Germany of 1940, 1941 and 1942 was not like that: and in Rotenburg-am-Fulda there was a preponderance of 'Grands Blessés' who, although passed unfit for further military service by the International Red Cross, were still waiting for the day when their captors would relent and let them go home.

What was especially cruel was that there had been one attempt at repatriation the year before, in September 1941. Arranged on the initiative of the Red Cross, a group of 'Grands Blessés' had been sent in hospital trains to the French port of Rouen at the mouth of the River Seine to be collected and taken across the Channel to England and freedom. But for some obscure reason, and without any warning, they were sent back into Germany, and then into Poland of all countries. There they were left for months, to shiver and freeze in the midst of one of the worst winters of the war before being returned to camps in Germany – including Rotenburg.

Many of the prisoners at Rotenburg had been on that abortive expedition to Rouen. Naturally they were bitter; and there were those who had little or no faith in the future, for they could not see then how the Allies were ever going to win the war, or how they could capture enough German prisoners to balance the overwhelming numbers of British and Commonwealth captives. Furthermore, the Americans had not yet become a factor in these calculations.

This was not what Geneva had intended, but statesmen before the war had not foreseen the Nazis' behaviour and intransigence in tearing up the rules of diplomacy.

The camp at Rotenburg was comparatively comfortable by POW standards. The building was dry and warm, but crowded and confined – so much so that it was literally possible to hide away from everybody else in the middle of the hundreds of other prisoners for days at a time – and many did.

Surrounding the main building was a large area of ground, compared to the confines of Spangenberg's 'top camp'. The whole of this was enclosed in a cocoon, a double fence of barbed wire about 10 ft thick and 15-20 ft high.

At each corner of the camp area, and at intervals in between, were sentry-boxes on high wooden stilts, 20–30 ft above the ground, giving an overall view of the camp inside – the same pattern as those seen in countless photographs and films of wartime Germany. Each sentry-box could accommodate one or more soldiers who, armed with a rifle or Mg 34 machine-gun, and searchlight, had a telephone connected to the Kommandantur in the German side of the camp, so that complete security could be maintained.

Food was, as always, of paramount importance. In Rotenburg we were divided into messes and fed from a central cookhouse. I never did eat any other way whilst I was a prisoner. There were other camps, however, where, because of size and numbers, the prisoners were left to fend for themselves in small groups. Some preferred to live that way, for if their elected cooks, fellow prisoners, officers and soldiers, were ingenious and careful they could eat with more variety than in a communal gathering such as we had in Rotenburg.

Sleep was of next importance. My first dormitory was in one of the large schoolrooms on the first floor, packed with thirty or more bunks arranged in closely ordered rows, with a few wooden tables and chairs in between them. My own bunk or, rather, my share of a two-tier bunk, was the upper half, 5 ft from the floor, and with my lame leg it was not at all easy to climb up. The lower bunk was occupied by an officer older than the others – a quartermaster called Weeks – 'Pop' Weeks – a pleasant but fussy little man, who walked very quickly and was always hurrying for some reason or other, particularly at meal-times when he literally ran to get to the eating-hall. His only real fault was his snoring. I was too tired to notice it that first night after the journey from Ober Masfeld; but on the second night I suddenly awoke to find myself the target for a barrage of books, and boots even, all aimed at my neighbour sleeping in the bunk below and snoring his head off. My companions were a mixed bag of army doctors, a dentist, and some Australians and New Zealanders. Their attitude to Weeks was uncompromising, and they were not too concerned about me. This snoring of Weeks was not to be tolerated. After the hail of missiles – he had obviously been hit by someone's boot – he grunted and stopped snoring, and the room settled down to an uneasy – and never quite silent – quiet rhythm of heavy breathing, and the rustle of human bodies at rest.

Those first few days were the most lonely and miserable I ever spent in prison, and I longed to be back at Spangenberg with my Commando friends, or at Rennes with the soldiers and sailors I had left behind me in that little haven of captivity in friendly France.

Prisoners at Rotenburg were kind and helpful but they had seen it all before – the new arrival and his tale of capture. After a few days of questioning they soon lost interest and returned to their own preoccupations. Their only interest really, and somewhat naturally, was in themselves and their own existence – of resignation and hidden despair.

Their attitude of mind then really reflected the conduct of the war. Depressed though we were at having been caught at St Nazaire, we had a different outlook, for a few months back we had been party to the slow recovery then taking place in Britain from the early defeats of the war. The formation of the Commandos had indeed been one of the first outward signs of the country's fight back. Churchill himself had used us to this end. Defeats there still were and more were to come, but we had seen the Battle of Britain being won, we had seen the modest victories at Vaagso and the Lofoten Islands; and at St Nazaire we had caught the Germans badly off balance. We knew that they were not invincible, as it had seemed in 1940, and we were not frightened of them – we were only wary and perhaps quietly condescending.

There were those in prison who recognised this rebirth of the Allied war effort, but there were others who were resentful and critical. Especially the 'Crows'. Life in POW camps was divided into those who could see no future, the 'Crows', and those who never gave up, never gave in, and who performed some of the most hazardous escapes to freedom ever recorded. I do not know if there are any statistics, but for every successful escaper there were untold dozens of attempts by officers and soldiers who, undeterred by discovery, betrayal, even, and recapture, tried again, and again, and again, to escape. In Rotenburg we were from every walk of life, and from countries all over the world. We still maintained military discipline, slightly casual at times, but when it was necessary, and in defiance of our captors, we could and did make every effort to show our non-acceptance of their domination. Strangely enough they recognised this attitude: on more than one occasion when I was in hospital at

Rennes I was asked, 'Why do you British fight us? Together we could beat the world,' to which I replied, 'We don't want to conquer the world.' They shook their heads disbelievingly. The fact that most of the map of the world was then coloured red was probably the reason for their disbelief, and there were then no signs in Britain that this red was to disappear fast, not increase.

Many years after the war was over, an older soldier, a veteran of the First World War, said to me: 'What I don't understand, dear boy' – he always called me that in a slightly patronising and superior manner – 'is what it was really like to be captured, to be a POW? Having to live – to exist even? What I have never appreciated was what your day-to-day life was really like . . .'

This is where telling my story becomes more difficult; for there I was at last in an ordinary established prison camp. I was not going to be moved about from hospital to hospital in France and Germany. I was not going to be able to observe the life lived by the ordinary Germans. I was about to live a life of drudgery, some excitement, some disaster and acquaintance with death, and curiously, to those who have never experienced such an existence, a life of despair that was yet leavened with great humour and a comradeship never to be experienced again.

I slowly came to adjust myself to this new life, and to recognise that survival and patience was the name of the game. For me, the first priority was to regain recovery of movement, and mobility. I remember being told to stop limping: 'It doesn't impress anyone and it only makes you conspicuous in the eyes of Germans.' The fact that my adviser was well over 6 ft tall, wounded in the head, but to all visible signs unharmed and very good looking did not impress me, but in a secret way I realised that he had made a point. His name was Howard Oliver, a gunner, and a 'card'. As I rapidly became more mobile I lost most of my limp.

I arrived at Rotenburg in the late autumn and the surrounding forest and hills were lovely in their autumnal colours. The weather was glorious and I soon came to enjoy watching the non-stop round of hockey and cricket matches – somewhat strange games which had been adapted to the confines of the area available to us. Hockey seemed the most popular, and although it was never my game, I hobbled around watching the everlasting matches, not really caring who won.

Soon, however, winter arrived and everyone started cocooning themselves in old overcoats, jerseys and scarves against the piercing cold.

The cricket season came to an end – true to form – and the wet tennis balls were dried out ready for the next season. For tennis balls soaked in pails of water were the substitute for cricket balls. No matter how good the batsmen (and some were of minor county standard) no one could really hit a wet tennis ball far enough for a six – right out of the prison compound. If they hit a ball into the wire another wet tennis ball was readily available from the pail of water and play continued. But with the onset of winter, life withdrew into the building and prisoners mostly returned to their books and study.

It was whilst watching a game of hockey that I first noticed a prisoner who was to become a close friend and confidant. Older than me, and with a neat military look about him, he was of medium height, had broad shoulders and was very strong. He had an air of authority and arrogance which distinguished him from the others and, as I was to discover, he had a contempt – hatred even – for our captors. I found this refreshing and in keeping with our recent training in Scotland and England. He was another Campbell, the nephew of the diplomat Ronald Campbell.*

David was one of twins, a captain in The Black Watch who had been cut off with his battalion at St Valéry. He already wore the Military Cross. Ever since his capture he had been digging and burrowing his way to freedom, only to be recaptured each time. His undaunted spirit and almost schoolboyish outlook on

---

* Later Sir Ronald Campbell, our Ambassador in Cairo. See also footnote on p.111.

life made him one of the camp personalities. His curiosity and
interest in the newly formed Commandos brought us together
and he introduced me to his circle of friends. Then, welcome of
welcomes, he arranged a bunk for me in his dormitory room.
I had nothing in common with my early room mates and wel-
comed the prospect of a smaller room with its double bunks
which lined the sides of my new quarters. The occupants were
more characteristic of the nature and purpose of Oflag IX AZ
and its 'Grands Blessés', for out of sixteen, four were minus an
arm or leg, two were partially paralysed, one was ill with cancer,
one was without some fingers, two were doctors – one from
South Africa and one from Australia – and the rest were disabled or lame in some form or other.

Again I was given a top bunk – the occupant beneath me was a
Welsh Guardsman who had lost an arm in the fighting in 1940:
Billy Winnington, or to give him his proper title, Sir Francis
Winnington, Bt., a great walker who would do hundreds of
circuits of the camp wire perimeter each week – flapping his arm
stump like a penguin as he tramped round and round for hour
after hour.

Here in this room was that same element of reserve and a
withdrawn attitude to life, but there was also a marked increase
in a sense of gaiety and fun – we mocked each other with a cruel
and ruthless disregard for niceties. Sympathy was never evident. There was something else – these men were younger than
the Australians and New Zealanders and years junior to old
'Pop' Weeks, the quartermaster. This division by age was a
general pattern in the camp and meant that in our room we were
all in our early twenties and early thirties – subalterns and
captains.

The field officers were grouped together in small rooms on
the next floor up – the 'Senior Officers' Quarters' so called, with
a few colonels and a brigadier. The Brigadier, Claude Nicholson, was commanding the British forces at Calais when it fell to
the Germans on 26 May 1940 after several days' severe fighting.
But he and his force of Green Jackets had held on long enough

to stop the German 10th Panzer Division from advancing northwards to cut off the BEF, thereby helping towards the successful evacuation of Dunkirk. This began a few days later and lasted for over a week, during which time 338,226 men were evacuated to England across the Channel, including 139,111 Frenchmen.

Nicholson was sacrificed together with his 20,000 troops and went with them into captivity. He was to die later in Rotenburg, but that tragic event did not take place until the following year, 1943.

I had already been allocated to a mess for meals and, despite my junior rank, I was invited to join a group of field officers – mostly regular soldiers who, had they not been captured, would by then have been many ranks senior.

And so the pattern of life at Rotenburg was set. It was a new camp with a mixture of prisoners not to be found anywhere else at that time, for it was full of wounded prisoners, padres and doctors. Winter had now set in and 'Appels' were allowed to proceed as fast as everyone wanted, both prisoners and guards. For cold is a great leveller – and cold it became – the cold of Central Europe – never far above freezing and often well below.

Those of us who had been captured on raids, or had been shot down, were issued with old army greatcoats looted from the great dumps of stores left behind by the army during the fighting in 1940, or sent to us by the Red Cross. Most of us wore balaclava helmets, knitted with loving care by our own relatives, or by the untiring Red Cross ladies back home, and sent out to us in what we called 'Clothing Parcels' as distinct from the precious 'Food Parcels'. We looked like, and were little removed from, tramps. Although a military presence was there, we had no way of showing it except in our attitude to each other, and we showed respect where it was due, particularly to the Senior British Officer.

The SBO was a Lieutenant-Colonel who had risen from the ranks. Lieutenant-Colonel Kennedy of the East Surrey

Regiment was a soldier, complete, from the way he wore his
forage cap – dead straight and central – to the creases in his well-
worn battledress trousers, and with the distinct shine on his army
boots; always 'on parade', but pleasant. We respected the way
he handled himself with the Germans – he was never ingratiat-
ing, as some were – and was always doing his best to represent
the camp's interests, limited though they were, and protesting
strongly when the Germans overstepped themselves.

I don't know why, but he was nicknamed 'Mops'. It sounds
contradictory because he was not the actual Senior British
Officer at Rotenburg. Apart from Brigadier Claude Nicholson,
there was a full colonel and a handful of other lieutenant-
colonels. But someone had to do the job of representing the
hundreds of officers. It was the same for other camps. These
senior officers, despite their own frustrations and a sense of
helplessness in captivity, were prepared to sacrifice what little
privacy was available to them, and take on the responsibility of
command, and between captor and captive act as go-between.
These men were respected, revered even, particularly by the
junior ranks and NCOs, for the way in which they constantly
reminded the Germans that, prisoners though we were, we were
still soldiers and that we were protected by the Geneva Convention.

Although I was not witness to the soldiers' camps, I am told
that the same pattern of discipline obtained there. In a huge
camp at Lamsdorf in Eastern Silesia there were some 50,000
British soldier prisoners. Separated from their own officers,
except for a MO and a padre, they were commanded by a
Regimental Sergeant-Major whose turnout would have graced
any regimental parade ground. His leather shone like glass and
his discipline would have been a credit to a Guards Depot.

These men held us together. I never saw them flinch and if it
had not been for them, the British Army would have been the
poorer.

David Campbell had already made his mark in Rotenburg and

previously in the early skirmishing both in the Maginot Line in France and in the fighting before St Valéry, south of Dunkirk.

When we met he was an established nuisance and there were those who protested at his insolent attitude, for they feared that his behaviour, and that of others like him, would lead to reprisals – for it had done so in previous camps.

It was during the late autumn of 1942 that I grew closer to David Campbell. He was a tough, arrogant Scot. He was restless and aggressive, a determined would-be escaper, kind and generous, but an unequivocal hater of captivity and our captors.

We were all aggressive in our own different ways, but Campbell was exceptionally so. I often thought that if he had concentrated his energies a little more on anonymity to help him escape, rather than draw attention to himself as a 'Goon* baiter', he might have been home and dry and 'escaped' before I was even captured. But no one I met in prison gave me more confidence and faith in the belief that escape was possible.

After Campbell had been captured at St Valéry in 1940 he endured the same miserable experience as thousands of others; he walked from northern France into Germany – along hundreds of miles of dusty roads – in the sun of that hot summer with little food, little to drink and with the depression of shattering defeat.

At Rotenburg autumn had passed – with the unbelievably beautiful changing colours of the forest – and then Christmas came. There was little food, certainly there were no geese getting fat; but it was Christmas-time, and life took on a mistletoe atmosphere. There was plenty of snow and we were living in the middle of a forest of Christmas trees.

The cooks were ingenious: Christmas dinner was a stew of beef and vegetables†, and potatoes as always, but filling. One survivor has told me that we had Christmas puddings – sent to

---

* POW slang for a German sentry.
† Also from our Red Cross parcels.

us by the Red Cross – I don't remember any. We did, however, have a miraculous cake made from the combined supplies of Bemax, margarine and raisins from our Red Cross parcels.

But I can never forget the loneliness of that Christmas afternoon. After we had eaten, the bridge players went off to their eternal games – mostly the older majors and colonels.

Poker, however, was equally absorbing and I knew how to play the game, or so I thought. But playing poker with Australians can be a rough ride. I tried, and although I knew the basic rules, I lost the equivalent in IOUs of all my pay saved up in my bank at Cox's & King's in London – all of 11 shillings a day, but with no interest accruing. Some £200 or more – all I had in the world. But poker is poker and I learned; and ultimately won most of it back.

There is one other memory of Christmas 1942. And that concerns a Christmas card. There was only one. The artist was a New Zealander, a brother of Greene Armitage, the famous surgeon. A good watercolourist, he painted a Christmas card showing our camp in the valley of the Fulda and sent it on behalf of us all to King George VI and Queen Elizabeth. The valley formed a natural V in the landscape and cunningly he so painted the view that the valley portrayed a symbolic V for Victory – but the German censors let it through undetected.

Those few days of Christmas were otherwise unmemorable and no one escaped. No one was punished. We lived or existed in a limbo of quiet depression and cold and hunger.

With the advent of New Year, life ground on and there was very little to do except read and sleep. If I had thought more about it, I would have used the time to study, hopefully for a university degree, or for chartered accountancy. Before the war I had worked for one of the oldest firms on the Stock Exchange, Joseph Sebag. I had been in the 'House' for three years and I knew my way about the market fairly well. Contemporaries of mine from those days are today senior partners of their firms. If I had returned from captivity with accountancy qualifications in addition to my City background, I would have probably been a stockbroker to this day. But I was too preoccupied then with other plans.

Meanwhile my reading increased into areas never thought possible before. At first my library was limited to novels and biographies. But after a time I turned to works by D.H. Lawrence, Tolstoy and Joyce and was introduced by Gerard Brett to the poems of Herrick. I devoured Lawrence's writings and especially his letters. Then *War and Peace* took me days to absorb – and I read it right through again; for at that time, the parallel was all too close to make it just a historical novel – it was our very life. There, only a few hundred miles away, were Russians fighting for their lives again, only this time against the Germans. Moscow was very near to the front line and the war maps in the German newspapers showed all the place-names from Tolstoy's marvellous epic.

The advent of winter, and the bitter cold, constituted a closed season for escape. At least I had no knowledge of any attempts to get away at that time; although later, I learned that reconnaissances were being made by the inveterate escapers in the camp, and particularly by David Campbell. It was not in his nature to sit still for very long, and although the temperatures outside were ranging down below zero, successful attempts had been made in previous winters.

14

Escapers: Nearly All

It was not until late in January 1943 that I first became aware of preparations for a major escape.

The plan was devised by Australians and New Zealanders, including two mining engineers from Australia. The whole operation was given priority, and backing from the camp's resources, under the command of the Officer in Charge of Escaping, Major Geoffrey MacNab*, an Argyll and Sutherland Highlander.

This effort was unique, for, unlike the larger camps, where several attempts were being made at any one time, this effort was to be concentrated to ensure speed with the utilisation of all available resources. As many prisoners as possible were mobilised to cover the actual digging of a tunnel and to support the escapers with forged documents, maps, food and clothing. For all had to be co-ordinated ready for the ultimate 'break' scheduled for Anzac Day on 25 April.

Despite the close confines of the camp and the hundreds of prisoners there the attempt had so far been kept a complete secret. The leaders of the escape had already dug down through the ground floor level of the building, in the gymnasium; down through the cavity in the walls, and foundations some 20 ft into the sub-soil. Then, striking out from the building towards the River Fulda, which lay a quarter of a mile away, the tunnel was to pass under some allotments which were built on reclaimed land adjoining the barbed wire perimeter.

The entrance was cunningly hidden by the panelling of the wall of the gymnasium and partially hidden by a radiator. The

* After the war he was promoted to Brigadier and knighted for his services.

entrance led into a small chamber just large enough to accommodate one person, and, from that, led to the head of a vertical
shaft some 20 ft deep, from which the actual tunnel then started
on its way towards the break-out point 75 yds away. The
tunnellers, six of them, had made wonderful progress, but it
was too much of a project for only a handful of prisoners. It was
at this point that the escape committee decided to step up the
effort, and that the team should be increased in numbers. It was
also decided that the 'diggers' of the tunnel should be divided
into shifts, working throughout each day. The new target date
for the break-out was the new moon in the month of June, when
there would be little light. The plan was now enlarged to involve
some fifty officers, who would 'break' under cover of dark, and
who would then split up, and make their way to freedom singly,
in pairs, or in small groups.

Although I was still lame, I was selected by David Campbell
to be one of the fifty would-be escapers. I was also to be one of
his team of diggers of five men. David was then recognised as
one of the most efficient tunnellers in the business, and to be
included in his team was something of an honour. He had been
taught to 'dig' by fellow POWs, Captain D.J. 'Jim' Rogers, a
distinguished mining engineer, and a Colonel 'Bob' Simpson, in
previous escape attempts.

I say I was lame: with a bullet still lodged in my right knee I
was lame and still am, but from hopping on my comparatively
good leg – there was shrapnel still there, but not in the joint –
my progression improved daily. To join the tunnellers was a
challenge; I had to force my legs into small spaces and thereby
break down the adhesions which would not normally have
succumbed. It is extraordinary what the human frame will take
if forced. I was lame, but there were others without limbs who
could shame the average uninjured man – and did so. If I was to
join the escape team I had to adjust and use the uninjured parts
of my body to compensate. After all, Long John Silver – who
must surely have been based on fact – was as quick on his one leg
as the other pirates on their two.

The other members of the team had been involved in previous attempts, and some were 'miners' of experience. I, on the
other hand, was a complete beginner. I also had difficulty in
moving in such small spaces as the beginnings of the underground tunnel – the vertical shaft and the actual tunnel were
approximately 22 in. wide and 18 in. high.

As soon as 'Appel' was finished each morning, digging
started. Entering the tunnel at approximately nine o'clock we
would dig for four hours or more until about one o'clock in the
afternoon. We would be relieved by another team of diggers
who continued tunnelling until the early evening. They would
then have to get out of the tunnel to get ready for the evening
roll-call, which took place at about seven o'clock. This routine
depended on strict timing and security. To succeed we had to
avoid creating any alarms, or distracting the Germans from
their day-to-day routine. There were alarms, but not during
those early weeks of digging.

There were three teams of diggers. And we were pro-
grammed so that if our team was on the morning shift, we would
not go down until the next afternoon, leaving the other two
teams to complete the afternoon dig and the next morning dig.
In this way we maintained variation and an interest in the
project, for experience of previous attempts had shown that, in
addition to the urgency, and the risk of discovery, if the digging
teams got tired – and it was very tiring work – they lost efficiency and became careless.

The progress of the tunnel varied with the subsoil we encountered. Because it was mostly sand, we would have made
fast progress had it not been for the danger of flooding. The
initial tunnelling was slow because it involved the construction
of small chambers in the tunnel in which we could just turn
round and in which we loaded the disposal boxes and bags onto
the little sledge which I pulled back down the tunnel, with a
home-made rope, to the foot of the shaft. The chambers were
also used as rest points. Progress, however, soon speeded up so
that we were tunnelling along at about 6 ft a day.

The faster we tunnelled, however, the larger became the problem of disposing of the soil or 'spoil' which we had dug out. Right from the start, the 'spoil' was packed into the discarded cardboard Red Cross food boxes. A 'Red Cross box' was an integral part of a prisoner-of-war's life, and was carried everywhere as he walked about the camp taking his bits of food with him. These boxes also had a variety of household uses and were accepted by the Germans as part of the daily scene. Once the 'spoil' had been packed into a box – a box could carry 20 lb in weight – it was hauled back along the tunnel to the shaft, pulled up by 'Sam' Parker* and stored to wait until the end of the dig. When the entrance to the tunnel was opened by those outside in the gymnasium, and once the diggers had been helped out, the 'spoil' was carried, box by box, by prisoner couriers, carefully but speedily through the camp building, up several flights of stairs into the large attic rooms in the roof where it was stowed away under the eaves inside the roof itself.

As the speed of tunnelling increased there would be fifty or more boxes ready for disposal at the end of each shift. If digging was difficult and slow, the disposal boxes would be that much fewer to get rid of. To move such large quantities of earth necessitated a meticulous schedule, not only for the carriers, but for those who had to reconnoitre the route, or, as we called it, 'to stooge' it for them. For there were always Germans about and their security guards within the camp never gave any warning as to their whereabouts. We had to institute a watch on them that had to be 100 per cent efficient. One mistake and the whole tunnel was at risk of being discovered.

Once the courier had got rid of his 'spoil', he then had to make his way back to an assembly point where his empty box was taken from him and held ready for return to the tunnel at the completion of the 'run'. The courier then returned to the

---

* Captain F.A.V. Parker, Rifle Brigade (now Green Jackets), who had been captured at Calais in 1940. A very large officer and a first-class cricketer who played for Hampshire.

gym for another box of earth to take up to the roof for disposal.

And so it went on until all the 'spoil' had been hidden away in the roof. There were some dozen or more couriers at any one time and they worked at great speed, and were never once stopped, or suspected, by the Germans.

Once we diggers had vacated the main tunnel we dressed again in our normal clothes, climbed up the shaft, and were helped out of the entrance into the gymnasium; and quickly made our way to the showers. There we had to remove all signs of dirt, sand and earth, swill it down the drains, dress again and mingle with the rest of the camp.

While we were doing this the new team would be entering the tunnel; then, allowing themselves to be closed in by the organisers, they would be left to continue the dig where we had left off. The change-overs were reduced to a fine art. They took a matter of minutes only. We relied completely on the efficiency and speed of the organisers, and of the 'stooges'; for had a German guard walked into the gymnasium during the change-over, the result would have been catastrophic and *very* dangerous. While we were digging, a great deal of work was being done by an efficient, cheerful and well-organised back-up of other prisoners who, either because they were not fit, or because of age or illness, had no wish to try to escape. They were busy every day preparing maps, identity cards and other essential documents, and clothes and food, for every one of the escape team.

Taking them in that order: an escaping prisoner had to have an up-to-date, and current, escape plan, and story. He had to pose either as a foreign worker, of which there were millions in Germany in those days, a traveller, or a businessman from, say, an occupied country – not German unless the escaper could speak perfect German – and a few of us could. Any one of these aliases meant that he had to have the several documents then required in wartime Germany to justify movement. An 'Ausweis' (exit permit), a work permit, an identity card, preferably with a photograph, and a letter or letters of reference. This documentation would have to stand close scrutiny by not only the police, the army, but worst of all by the Gestapo, who were everywhere. In addition an escaping prisoner had to have maps of sufficient quality, and detail, to assist him in finding his way across Germany, into Switzerland, or France, to Spain or Sweden. No one that I know ever tried to escape eastwards to Russia; for that was considered to be too dangerous, and with the additional risk of getting involved in the violent fighting of those days.

Maps were copied from other maps which had either been stolen from our hosts or had come from airmen who had been shot down. There were other sources of supply from our own military contacts back in London. To name a few: certain gramophone records – in those days 78s – when split open contained not only maps of the highest quality, but documents as well, later in the war made out in our own names and identities. Tins of food in 'marked' parcels had double skin linings in which were hidden more maps and documents; then there was the additional source of supply from incoming air-men; as well as maps, compasses and other vital escape material miraculously escaped detection and were put to good use by the 'old lags' or 'Kriegies'* as they were called.

The maps were painstakingly copied by hand by our fellow prisoners on to sheets of white paper which were then smeared with margarine or 'speise' – cooking fat – and baked in the camp ovens to dry off the fat and thereby make them waterproof. To supply fifty would-be escapers with maps meant copying hundreds and hundreds of sheets of paper covering routes from the heart of Germany into the Ruhr and westward to France, or through Berlin to the north and the Baltic, or directly south to the Swiss frontier. In my case, I intended to escape posing as a French soldier prisoner-of-war moving to a new place of work, for there were thousands of French soldier-prisoners then working in Germany. I was dark-haired and did not look

---

* 'Kriegie': POW slang for *Kriegsgefangener*, prisoner-of-war.

particularly British. I could speak fairly fluent French – albeit
not very grammatically – but at that time certainly enough to
pass most German sentries. My uniform was partly that which I
had worn on leaving hospital in France, and partly salvaged
from the hospital in Ober Masfeld. It consisted of a khaki jacket
as worn by the French regular soldiers until the collapse of
France; the breeches were those that I had been given on leaving
hospital in France, as were my puttees and French boots. I was,
therefore, little or no problem for the Escape Committee. There
were others, however, who required a complete set of civilian
clothes, a cap or hat, a briefcase, shoes – not boots. To meet this
requirement, and many others like it, meant tailoring suits of
clothing to fit each individual. Material was a problem, but
it was solved by shaving our dark blue and dark grey army
blankets with safety razors until they were sufficiently thin to
work, and which on a cursory examination passed as worsted.

The officer in charge – a captain in the Newcastle Scottish
Regiment, Johnny Webster – was a master tailor and had been
badly wounded in 1940. With his willing assistance and skill he
cut dozens of suits for the strangest clientèle ever to be tailored
by hand. Under his supervision I made a suit myself, to be used
by someone else. Hand-stitched, and with buttons – where they
came from I don't remember – the whole was an impressive and
fair imitation of the real thing.

For those of us who were to walk most of the way to freedom –
500-1000 miles – there was an allocation of food which had been
hoarded from Red Cross parcels and bought from fellow POWs
with our camp money: chocolate, sugar, oatmeal, and a form
of cake, more like cattle food, made from these ingredients
and Bemax, and cooked into small squares. These were stored
away pending our escape.

Geoffrey MacNab kept a cheerful and benevolent, albeit
strict, control of the entire operation; and we accepted his
decisions without question. Out of the 500 officers in the camp
approximately fifty others, who would not break out, were
engaged in working on our behalf. They did so without com-

plaint. If there were any protests from the rest in the camp, they were immediately squashed by MacNab and his Committee with, in some cases, the threat of court martial at the end of the war. So efficient and careful was the Escape Committee that the Germans suspected nothing. At least, so we thought, for there were no searches and no outward sign of increased security on their part.

Day followed day and the face of the tunnel receded farther and farther away from the camp until we had dug and excavated some 50 yds of tunnel 15–20 ft underground, and far out under the allotment away from the wire. We suffered delays, mostly because of sudden and dangerous falls of earth and sand, which the diggers at the face had to shore up with wooden pit-props to prevent the possible collapse of the whole project. The wood for the props was obtained from each prisoner in the camp who had to give up one of the bed-boards from his bunk. A bed-board was about 4 ft long and 6 in. wide and lay on the skeleton structure of our double-tiered bunks with our straw palliasses and blankets laid on top of them. This levy formed the basic objection from the others, resulting in the protests I have described. The levy was imposed with strict impartiality, and the bed-boards were sawn and reduced in size into small props, just like those used in coal mines. They were taken down the tunnel at the beginning of each new dig to be installed as the digging continued.

March arrived, and we were behind schedule, but we were not too concerned, for everything else was progressing as planned. Suddenly however the weather changed. It rained hard and continuously for days on end. We were already very near the water-table and with the rain the tunnel came under immediate strain, and in great danger of collapsing altogether.

Our own particular team was down below one morning, and digging went on as before. Captain David Campbell was working at the face, Captain P.F. 'Pup' Arkwright, 16/5th lancers, and Captain John Hamilton Parker, The Prince of Wales Volunteers, called 'Screwpicket' because he was so thin, were strung out behind him in the tunnel's loading chambers.*I was at the beginning of the tunnel hauling away at the sledge on which were boxes and bags of earth, to load them into the bucket which 'Sam' Parker then hauled up to the head of the shaft, where he stored them by his side for the next disposal run. It was a miracle that 'Sam' could ever squeeze his vast frame into the tunnel, let alone work for hours on end, in a crouched position, virtually entombing himself with the boxes of earth he stored around him.

Suddenly there was a low rumble. A rush of air blew out the lamps – and, after a second of shock and surprise, we realised that there must have been a major fall, near the face. It seemed as if the entire tunnel had collapsed. After a terrifying wait, and silence, we found that we were still intact but in a very dangerous position. Campbell and Arkwright were virtually cut off from the rest of us and heavy falls of earth and sand were blocking large sections of the tunnel. After a few minutes we restored contact with Campbell and Arkwright, and started to clear the fallen earth so that they could slowly and carefully wriggle backwards towards us and safety.

As we busied ourselves with the problem of survival, and of saving the tunnel, we had time only to act, and talk afterwards. Then, unexpectedly, we received a signal from the top of the shaft; we were to stop all digging and movement – there was an alarm. This often happened, and we were not too concerned at first, rather we were much more worried about the tunnel and hoped that after a few minutes of waiting we would be given the all-clear so that we could continue the usual rescue operation. But there was no all-clear.

There we were, in what was left of the tunnel, with no light, and with our air supply noticeably deteriorating. The air was supplied through a crude hand-made pump which pushed fresh air to us through an air duct made of hundreds of powdered

* The other member of the team, Captain Charles Madden, 60th Rifles, could not dig because of his wounded leg.

milk tins soldered together in lengths and joined into one long
supply line to the diggers at the face of the tunnel. We dared not
use the pump with our captors nearby, but we had already built
up a reserve of fresh air which would keep us conscious – but not
for ever. We whispered to each other, to check that we were all
right; but as we lay there, we began to feel the cold and the
pressures of nature. There was no alternative but to pee into our
bottles. David Campbell reminds me that we held the bottles
against our bodies, using the warmth of their contents, until
they were too cold. Then we had to pour it away on to the floor
of the tunnel where we lay. The miracle was that the air,
although getting steadily worse, was still sufficiently clear to
keep us awake. As we lay there, we wondered what could have
happened. It was certainly nothing to do with us, for had the
Germans suspected anything wrong we would have heard all
about it by then.

We must have lain there for three or four hours. We were
hungry, we were very cold – we had few or no clothes on – and I
for one was increasingly fearful of what would happen if more of
the tunnel were to collapse on top of us.

At about 4.30 in the afternoon – we had been in the tunnel
since nine o'clock in the morning – we suddenly and unbelievably got a signal that all was clear. After a few seconds of blessed
relief and excited whispering to each other, we suddenly felt
cool fresh air from the open trap door to the tunnel, from which
we were literally dragged out, into the light of the gymnasium,
and the relief of more fresh air. How long we would have lasted
in the tunnel I do not know, but the relief of getting out of the
claustrophobic damp, mud and mess of the underground work-
ings was something I can never forget.

It was some minutes before we took in the fact that the faces
of several strangers were looking at us. Strangers who were just
as surprised as we were, as they gathered round us, and started
to ask questions in the unmistakable accents of Americans.
Unbeknown to us, just after we had started digging that morning, a group of 150 American officers arrived at the camp and

were brought into the gymnasium to be searched. This was normal practice for all new prisoners. The search had taken several hours and when it had finished the Americans were issued with blankets and palliasses and told that they were to sleep on the floor of the gymnasium.

Meanwhile the Escape Committee was helpless and, apart from the hasty signal flashed to us to stop digging, they could do nothing. They had been turned out of the gymnasium to be kept away from the new arrivals. I think they were more worried about this unexpected interruption than we were, although they had no idea then of the even greater danger we faced of being buried alive 15-20 ft down. Although we were pleased to see the Americans, and tried to explain what we had been doing, it was of considerable concern to us that the Americans were witnesses to the tunnel – which until then was a closely guarded secret, the precise location of which was not known even to the majority of our helpers. It was decided to close the tunnel for a few days, until life settled down again, but principally because we did not want the new arrivals to see any more than was absolutely essential. As much as we appreciated their concern at what they had seen, it was a case of 'what the eye doesn't see'.

During the next few days the Americans were moved out of the gymnasium into the sleeping quarters so that in our room we accommodated six more young and bulky officers. We tried to get hold of the ones we liked the look of and with whom we had already made friends. There were now eighteen of us in very small confines, but we were comparatively lucky, because although our room was small, in the larger rooms even more overcrowding had to be accepted until the gymnasium was cleared.

In the words of David Campbell:

Once the Americans were absorbed into the dormitory rooms in the camp, the gymnasium was free again. The tunnel was opened up. It was in a deplorable state. There had been another fall. The forward drive was blocked off. The whole area of the tunnel running under the road was flooded. The pump forward was blocked off by the fall; before we could do anything it had to be salvaged. Arkwright and I went down. The roof [of the tunnel] under the first ditch, short of the road, was cracked right across in several places, water dripped through at an alarming rate. It would not hold very much longer. We crawled on up to the fall.

Scraping away carefully we made a small hole in the soil at roof level. Immediately we were swamped by a rush of water which burst over us, to pour back down the tunnel. We managed to check it by building up [a barrier] again with Red Cross boxes of earth, to allow only a small gap, under the roof. Holding a lamp into this hole we surveyed a scene of stark desolation. Our shadows cast eerie figures on what appeared to be a bubbling sheet of water vanishing out of sight in inky blackness. This was caused, we saw, by water pouring from the roof. There was no sign of the further chamber. The ceiling dipped down a bit, about half-way out of sight [to the chamber], which hid it from view. The pump was in this chamber. There was nothing for it but to go in and get it.

Taking a deep breath, and holding the lamp at roof level, with my right hand, I slid over the wall into the water like a crocodile. Christ! It was cold. Still water always is. Scrabbling with my left hand I pulled myself along with about 6 in. to spare for my head. The further I went, the less the gap became until the water reached the roof. My light went under and went out. I checked. It was too cold to think, so I took a deep sniffling breath through my nose, pressed to the roof, and submerged totally, frantically clawing forward, with both hands on the floor. Fortunately the 'sets' [of pit props] were still holding so I got a good purchase, but I daren't put much pressure on them.

When I thought my lungs would burst, the roof level heightened, and my head was clear and above water. I had reached the forward chamber. Feeling round in the dark I felt the pump. Good! It was safe. I groped about the chamber, and touched a lamp in a special recess. Wonderful! There were matches too . . . By a sheer fluke I lit the lamp. Repairs would be needed here too . . . I had no more time because the lamp suddenly went out. I had forgotten that I was beyond the supply of air and was cut off by a freezing sheet of water. Clutching the pump, and taking the deepest breath I could, I started back through the water. Once or twice [the pump] stuck on pieces of 'set' but I got it through and emerged into both air and light to see Pup's face peering through the hole in the wall of earth. Within a few seconds Pup had the pump working. I was far too cold to help him so I crawled back and sent a message up to Ian [Bessell-Brown]* through Stewie and Parky who were waiting at the foot of the shaft. Ian ordered me out and sent 'Sam' Parker into the top chamber to pump air for Pup, Stewie and Parky. They did a hell of a good job and pumped most of the water out . . . which was sent back to the shaft, in a bucket and three large jam tins on the trolley cart, and hoisted up the shaft by a pulley and passed out for a 'run' for disposal in the wash house.

The next day was a Sunday, I remember, and a rest day for our team, so I was a bit disappointed when Ian found me walking round the yard with Billy Winnington, and said, 'The tunnel's fallen in. There is a gaping hole showing in the first ditch by the road outside the camp.' Whilst Ian organised an emergency 'stooge' operation with watchers, demonstrators and riot squads, I collected our team together; Ian Bessell-Brown and Tom Westly had their administration at fever pitch. Timber, Red Cross boxes, socks, stockings, a broom and a dustbin lid. As quickly as we could Ian, Pup, Fred Corfield and I crawled up to the fall.† Christ! we all muttered under our breath. It really was a fall. We stood up in a vast cavern. It was 4 ft across, 5 ft 6 in. wide and 9 ft high. The clear blue sky was visible through a jagged triangular hole 12 in. by 18 in. By the grace of God a large clod of turf [from the hole in the ground] was lying intact on top of the fall. Ian placed it on the dustbin lid, and holding it up, so that I could get the broom under it, then steadied by Pup and Ian, I raised it up and up towards the hole, hardly daring to breathe, and we eased it into place, turning the broom handle slightly to get the correct fit. The hole

*One of the leaders of the whole escape operation, a big cheerful Australian major.

† Fred Corfield was a burly New Zealand officer and was a great oarsman before the war.

was filled . . . Ian bent down quickly and lit our three lamps. Working quickly [he was well over 6 ft tall] he piled Red Cross box on top of box until they came level with the end of the broom handle which I was holding . . . more and more boxes of earth were packed in terraces up towards the roof . . . and slowly and surely we rebuilt the hole . . . The tunnel was saved! It took us three hours to do it, but we had been unaware of time. Often we had nearly burst out laughing hearing children talking gaily in the road, bicycle bells, dogs yapping, girls giggling and the camp noises of softball being played . . .*

Whilst David and the rest of the team were working in the tunnel, desperately trying to repair what had nearly been a disaster, I meanwhile had been left in the camp to act as 'stooge', and keep special watch from the music-room in the attic, so that I could look down on to the ditch, beside the road, where I could see the hole they were trying to fill. If there were any signs of German suspicions, and further danger, I was to pass a signal down to them to stop all movement and noise.

I was made 'stooge' for there were only a few of us who knew what had happened and that the hole existed. If others in the camp saw the hole someone was bound to show too much interest and alert the ever-suspicious Germans. Luckily, no one inside the camp noticed and the pedestrians, and the German sentry patrolling his beat some 6 yds from the hole, suspected nothing. As I watched, I literally prayed for those who were working underground to make haste. Suddenly out from the bowels of the earth a large piece of turf appeared and grew out of the hole as if made of 'instant' grass. From above, it seemed to fit immediately in place, but according to David, when the turf was pushed up and out of the hole it was pushed too far before it slowly subsided into place. The hole was no longer visible. David, in his usual malicious way, said, 'Had I been a dis-interested watcher, I would have preferred to see a German fall through and disappear'; but however funny that would have

* Quoted from an unpublished MS by David Campbell.

been at the time, it would have been the end of the tunnel.

As David said, 'The next few days were spent on urgent repairs.' Because of the damage, and delays caused by repairs, the Escape Committee decided to include yet another team of diggers in the attempt, and an American team joined us. Led by a young Texan, it consisted of six officers, making a total of over sixty officers who would make the break. With this added support the tunnel was soon pushing out again towards the break point. Tunnelling continued through May and June and we made good progress.

15

Death of the Polish Army

Suddenly, in the middle of June an extraordinary incident took place. It was to have world-wide repercussions for years afterwards, and even to this day it has never been resolved.

The German Army at this time was once again on the attack in Russia and was advancing eastward from Smolensk towards Moscow a few hundred miles away. The Germans had occupied the area for the whole of the previous winter, and as the weather improved and the snows melted, it was reported to the Germans by the Russians still living in the area that the bodies of thousands of Polish officers had been discovered in the forests there – near a Russian village called Katyn. This was reported immediately by Berlin radio, but Berlin propaganda was always highly suspect.

The first word we heard of this alleged atrocity was when the Germans asked the Senior Officer of our camp to nominate officer prisoners to go to Katyn and see what had been discovered there. Other POW camps were similarly approached. The initial reaction was one of suspicion, for everything the Germans did at that time had a propaganda content, and we treated the Germans with disbelief.

Eventually two reluctant officers – Lieutenant-Colonel van Vliet, US Army, senior American in the camp, and Lieutenant-Colonel Stevenson of the South African Army, a Signals officer – agreed to go to Katyn. They were flown east to Smolensk in military aircraft, and driven a few miles through the Russian forests to Katyn. Several days later these officers returned, and told us that they had seen the bodies of thousands of dead Polish officers lying in long shallow graves in the forest – they had all been shot in the back of the head. Despite decomposition it was still possible to identify their Polish uniforms, in which were their personal papers, and copies of newspapers dating back to 1940. Van Vliet and Stevenson were in a group of some 'ten Allied officers' who visited Katyn at that time – an event which was later described by a Dr M. Wodzinski, a Polish Army doctor, who was there as a representative of the Polish Red Cross. Wodzinski's report revealed the names of those officers for the first time, for the Germans had not used our comrades' rank and names, as we had feared, for their propaganda purposes. Wodzinski's report of the visit coincides in every detail with the report of the Allied officers themselves.

According to the *New York Times* dated 19 September 1950, van Vliet's report had been released the day before by the US Department of Defense, and the full text was read out at a session of the House of Representatives in Washington by Representative John E. Rankin the next day. It describes how van Vliet was taken with a group of fellow prisoners from an Oflag near Rotenburg 'to view the graves of the Polish Officers in Katyn Wood near Smolensk'.

Van Vliet reported that he did not proceed voluntarily to the place of the crime, and also refused to express an opinion (at that time) as to who was responsible for the massacre. He added that as far as he knew German propaganda never took advantage of his visit to Katyn. The report gave the names of other Allied prisoners-of-war who went to Katyn, including that of Colonel Stevenson. Van Vliet said that the rest of the group of Allied officers who visited Katyn also 'believed that the Russians did it'. From our point of view, prisoners in Rotenburg, we believed Stevenson and van Vliet.

However, because of the Allies' need to maintain friendly relations with Russia after the war, van Vliet's report was kept secret till 1950. For as General Bissell admitted to the Select Committee of the American Congress in 1952, 'If it had been publicised in 1945 when agreements for creating a United Nations Organisation reached at Yalta were being carried on in San Francisco, Soviet Russia might never have taken a seat in that International Organisation.'

In justifying his actions for designating van Vliet's report 'Top Secret', General Bissell said he was merely carrying out the spirit of the Yalta agreement. But Top Secret or no, reports like this have a habit of coming to the surface and it was on 18 September 1951 that the House of Representatives of the 82nd Congress of the United States unanimously adopted House Resolution 390 in respect of establishing 'a full investigation and study of all the facts, evidence and circumstances of the Katyn Forest massacre and international crime committed against the soldiers and citizens of Poland at the beginning of World War II'.

The Committee's first public hearing was held in Washington on 11 October 1951 and further hearings were held in 1952 in Washington, Chicago, London and Frankfurt-am-Main and again in Washington. They produced a monumental report in December of that year, 1952, which occupies 2366 pages, and which reports that the Committee 'unanimously finds, beyond any question of reasonable doubt, that the Soviet NKVD (People's Commissariat of Internal Affairs) committed the mass murders of the Polish Officers and Intellectual Leaders in the Katyn Forest near Smolensk, Russia'.

One last comment and some of the facts: 4143 bodies were exhumed from the seven mass graves seen by van Vliet and Stevenson. On the basis of further evidence the Committee reported that: 'we are equally certain that the rest of the 15,000 missing Polish Officers were executed in a similar brutal manner near Kharkov and that others were placed on barges and drowned in the White Sea.' To get some idea of what this terrible action meant – 15,000 officers is approximately the officer strength of over 30 divisions and support units or some 500 battalions of officer strength in modern army establishments.

I mention Katyn (some describe it as Katyn Wood) because it was part of the fabric of life of prisoners-of-war then and the despair, and sometimes revulsion, of that life in Germany in

1943. To mention Katyn to a Pole today is akin to talking to the British about the bombing of London – only more so. It was, and is, symbolic of part of a war in which more than fifty million people were killed, or died.

The reported incident had little evident effect on the rest of us at that time, but it confirmed our secret fears and realisation that we were captive in a world in which life was cheap – valueless in fact. It also brought home to us the seemingly hopeless mess of our situation if the war was to deteriorate further. 'What was it like, dear boy?' Indeed it was like that.

Apart from the increasing progress being made on the tunnel project, life in the camp followed a somewhat dull pattern, although there was, thank goodness, a continuing thread of humour to liven our days. The twice-daily 'Appels' were crucial to our daily lives, for everything was centred on these parades. They in turn produced some curious and unusual degrees of humour. For example, Michael Maude, an officer of the Innis-killing Dragoon Guards who had lost his leg in France, spoke very good German and acted as our 'Dolmetscher' – interpreter – between the German Command and the Senior British Officer. For no reason, one day, the German Senior Officer said in German: 'Herr Maude, wie viele Warme Brüder sind in diesen Lager?' (How many buggers are there in this camp?)

Maude's reaction to this curious question was one of hesitation as to how to translate such a question to Colonel Kennedy. The latter, seeing his hesitation, said in his gruff voice 'Come on, Maude, out with it, what's he want?'

Maude, playing for time, asked the German Commandant to repeat the question and again the German said, 'Wie viele Warme Brüder sind in diesen Lager?'

At this, Maude said to the Colonel, 'The commandant wants to know how many homosexuals there are in this camp.'

The Colonel expressed genuine surprise at such a suggestion and replied, 'Tell him we don't condone buggery in the British Army – I'll have none of that nonsense.' Whether or not his reply was completely true, the German did not retaliate, but the Commandant's expression showed his disbelief that in a close-knit community of over 500 officers there were not some who had homosexual tendencies.

One of the German officers – the oldest of all and a veteran of the First World War – was a Captain Count von Seckendorf who was called 'death on wheels' because of his curious gliding action as he paraded in front of us when counting the 'Appel'. He also wore the longest jackboots we had ever seen. He was very well-mannered and very obviously of the old German officer class, a member of the von Seckendorf family who were well known in Germany and had been close friends of Queen Victoria and Prince Albert. He was not a snob, but he had a curious respect for titles. As he walked down the ranks of the officers parading in front of him in rows of five, and he came to Viscount Tarbat (now the Earl of Cromartie) he would murmur 'guten morgen'. Again, as he came to Billy Winnington he offered a polite 'guten morgen'. To the dozen or so officers who had titles he showed this respect of knowledge of their antecedents, much to the amusement of the rest of us.

At about this time a group of Indian officers who had been captured in North Africa were brought into the camp and when the senior Indian complained of the cold and lack of heating he was told by the Germans that it was our fault, the British officers. At which the Indian drew himself up and said, 'Ah! but you don't seem to understand; we, too, are British officers, it is your fault, you Germans.'

On the subject of self-improvement and education I was flattered when some Indian officers asked me if I would help them to improve their English. I found some grammar books and an Oxford dictionary in the library and arranged to meet them each morning for an hour's tuition – there were about six of them. Alas! after a week it became increasingly evident that my schoolboy command of our syntax was not strong enough, and I tactfully withdrew under the guise of being too busy with my own studies – I never really could face the appeal in their eyes when we met and I knew that they knew that I had let them down. But I could never have faced the embarrassment of being found out, as a kind of BA (failed).

And so, one way and another, I had little time to brood. Reading, the non-stop poker school – they all took up time when we were not working on the tunnel.

With the advent of a late spring the weather had improved and the rain stopped. The sun rose in the sky, it grew warmer, and we were able to go outside again. The cricket season was officially opened, hockey continued as always, but that spring and summer a serious competitor in the shape of a new game captured our imagination.

There was already a small group of Canadian officers from the Dieppe raid at Rotenburg and together with the arrival of the 150 American officers their influence on our lives began to make its mark. Neither the Americans nor the Canadians, putting them in alphabetical order, knew much about cricket; and playground hockey, as we called it, was not really to their liking. Ice hockey, yes – we flooded the playground and let it freeze into a rough and ready ice rink – but it was now late spring. No, their real love was baseball. But baseball requires even more space than cricket. There is a variant played by the Canadians – it is called softball.

Softball is what its name suggests – a soft variant of a baseball; a large grapefruit-sized ball with the same stitching as the bullet-hard baseball – but hit it as hard as you can and if you can carry it 100 ft or so you ought to be playing Test Match cricket or in the World Series.

Softball caught on and immediately had a universal appeal. The Americans and Canadians obviously loved the attention they created and hammed it up to the limit. It was like the spring – and it was electrifying to the rest of us, and symbolic of the New World influence on the war. Even the German sentries were intrigued, for cricket was really too complicated – slow even – for their Teutonic tastes. Strangely there is no German game in the summer like cricket or baseball; tennis, yes; swimming, yes; but there is nothing in Germany or elsewhere in Europe to replace football when the summer comes.

Although cricket continued to hold its place in that summer in 1943, and wet tennis balls were constantly being driven into the barbed wire fences, it was really the year of softball. A softball 'World Series' was the outcome, and with great enthusiasm and support from the whole camp it was bitterly contested and finally won by the British Empire team – much to the disgust of the American and Canadian teams. Softball indeed!

The strong sun of a mid-European summer was another blessing in disguise, for it provided a natural cover for us, the diggers, who, spending day after day underground, were in danger of attracting attention by our pale thin faces. So the order went out, to sunbathe whenever one could and at the same time take advantage of the warmth the sun provided, and get as much sleep during the day outdoors as possible.

We also walked all we could, and each one of us in the escape team took every opportunity to exercise, and joined the inveterate walkers who spent days plodding round the perimeter of the camp.

It was not unusual to see prisoners walking at any moment of the day round and round the camp yard for hours on end, from early morning till late evening when we were locked up in the camp buildings for the night. Singly – those were mostly the professionals and all-weather walkers – and in twos and threes – no more – for there was not enough room, they beat a path in an anti-clockwise direction round and round in a never-ending promenade. Although we were underweight and hungry, we were very fit.

My leg improved all the time and my limp became less marked. Also I was able to join in the games. I was not much good at cricket, it never was my game. Softball was equally dependent on speed and that I had no longer. Hockey was better, but here I had to be careful for a flying hockey-stick on my knee could be very painful.

And so I mostly threw one of the rugby balls to David, and then tried to torpedo-throw the ball under instruction from two large Americans, a Captain 'Spud' Murphy, who had played college football for a Southern State university and another from Michigan State who had played 'end' for his college. The American football is much narrower than our rugby ball, but they could spin our larger rugby ball with accuracy and speed over greater distances than we knew how.

The main point of all this activity was that it was never-ending, except when it rained. Elsewhere in the camp a hundred and one activities were going on. I remember, quite clearly, one beautiful morning, waiting for a disposal run from the tunnel up into the attic of the roof, and looking out across the road to the river and listening to the camp life going on below me.

There was an interrupted clamour – not noisy – that was confined to the exercise yard, but in the camp building itself there was a steady drone, rising and falling with the sound of the camp orchestra at rehearsal, solo musicians practising – and my friend Gerard Brett with his beloved cello – seemingly so in keeping with his quiet character. In the distance, I could hear 'Sam' Parker with his trumpet; no Louis Armstrong he, but proficient. A piano was always being hammered, not always with much rhythm or in time. One of my sisters was an erst-while young concert pianist so I had heard better, but hammered it was. There was the eternal gramophone playing the latest records from home. There was the hammering of nails as the stage hands built the next 'props' for a camp concert. These 'prop men' were the only prisoners officially allowed to use tools for their work, and on trust, and their tools had to be handed back to the Germans every evening after use. There were other tools in the camp, however, hidden under floor-boards and in wall cavities. Tools manufactured by ourselves, or 'stolen' – 'lifted' was the word – from German workmen.

The noise inside the camp was unrelenting and must have

intrigued and constantly puzzled the German pedestrians passing by on the road outside. It was different from the noise emanating from a school: it was more varied and did not ebb and flow with school breaks or sound with the shrill screams and shouts of playtime; it continued fairly steadily through each morning until the so-called lunch-time and then quietened down for an hour or so after luncheon, to start again with the inevitable game of cricket or softball from mid-afternoon until supper and evening 'Appel' called halt.

In the tunnel, progress quickened, and after the American team had been shown what to do the 'face' advanced at an inexorable speed. We repaired the damage caused by the fall – then it was dig, dig, dig. We disposed of the 'spoil' in the roof. We copied our maps when not digging, we sewed our escape clothes and thought of nothing much else except how best to use the time left to us before we were ready to make the break.

16

A Traitor

All this time we had been closely aware of a prisoner who, despite his chatter, was suspected of being a *poseur*. He had an educated background and could speak more than one foreign language, but there was something wrong about his story – about his make-up. I first met him when I arrived at Spangenberg to find that the others from the St Nazaire raid had already marked him down, particularly so when he had claimed common heritage, as it were, with us. In other words, 'I am a Commando too.'

When I arrived in August 1942 he had already been questioned by the others, but as he claimed to have been recruited in the Middle East it was not easy to pin him down or check on his bizarre background. Unhappy about his claims, however, we spoke to General Fortune – but kind and fatherly as he was, he told us to do nothing – the Germans might harm the man – and he was after all a British soldier, or so he claimed.

When I was transferred to Rotenburg via Ober Masfeld, he turned up at Rotenburg, how or why no one knew. Months passed, and in a group of incoming POW officers was a young captain in The Black Watch, Sir George Dick-Lauder, who, when he saw our friend, identified him to us as one of the soldiers who had been captured in Crete.* He was next reported to have adopted the rank of lieutenant to avoid the hardship of being a soldier-prisoner. Strangely enough it was the other way round, for life as a soldier-prisoner often meant more freedom.

* Captain George Dick-Lauder wrote to me recently: 'I was captured in Crete in 1941. I do remember the man you wrote about and that he was not an officer, but after capture posed as one in the belief, I think, that as such he would have a more comfortable prison life.'

Also many soldier-prisoners worked on farms and they had better food than the officer POWs who were not allowed to work, and certainly had no freedom. Our friend, however, kept up his façade – gloried in it even.

However, his very presence in our midst was the one uncertain link in an existence which depended on complete and utter confidence in one another. There in the midst of a major escape attempt was this strange and unpopular little man who saw everything that was going on and even offered to help in the map department.

It was some time during this period that the American officers were moved away from our camp into a new prisoner-of-war compound which was being constructed elsewhere, with the exception of Colonel van Vliet who, feigning sickness, was allowed to stay behind, so that he could escape when the tunnel was complete. A remarkable thing happened at the Americans' departure which will always remain with those of us who had become friendly with them. As the 156 American officers paraded in the prison yard to be marched away to the railway station they suddenly came to attention and sang 'God Save the King' to us. It was the most touching and unexpected tribute and we cheered them all the way as they marched past the camp down the road towards the station. We had made many friends amongst these men, the first American officers to be captured in Africa in the war. We had taught them much about prisoner-of-war life but, in return, they had given us new spirit and a new confidence in the outcome of the future.

Meanwhile the tunnel grew longer and longer; and then came the time when it was nearly complete and we would be ready to break.

The tunnel was finished, but the Public Record Office, quoting the Directorate of Military Intelligence (WO 20) and WO 208/3293-4, reported after the war that the tunnel was 12 ft short of the planned break-out point. This was according to plan, for quite what would have happened had we gone ahead to break the tunnel then, and find we had another 12 ft to dig, with a queue of 60 officers crawling down behind us, is indeed a frightening thought, but there was no room for mistakes of such a nature. No, the 12 ft was intentional cover against discovery.

Unfortunately, however, the flooding and near-collapse of the whole tunnel had thrown us off schedule. Our programme was a whole moonlight phase too late – or so argued the experts. I did not agree. My training at Lochailort had been based on 'action this day'. Delay could only court disaster – no matter the risks – what was the whole thing about anyway? It was all based on risk, and there could be no point in extending the element of risk. Or so I argued when the whole team met in secret one evening to debate what to do.

However, I was too junior, and in the eyes of the other escapers, many older and undoubtedly more experienced, I was too impatient, and anyway 'who is this young officer – who are these Commandos?' Some of them called us 'Glamour Boys'! And some asked 'what was so different about them – special forces indeed!' I was overruled.

And so it was decided to close down everything until a few weeks later when the moon phase darkened the night skies. I was too junior to argue, but from what David Campbell has written, some of the others were also uneasy and not so confident of our self-imposed delay.

Meanwhile the camp routine continued as before and we sunbathed in the blazing heat, played cricket and softball each afternoon and poker in the evening. The bridge schools continued as if nothing had changed. To them nothing *had* changed – bridge was all-absorbing and was not to be disturbed by a group of people who were planning to escape – only to be recaptured the next day, or at the most, days later. After all 'Hearts are trumps'.

It had been a lovely June day and as night fell we went to bed as usual. At one o'clock the next morning the whole camp exploded, and with shouts, and more shouts, and the crashing of rifle butts on doors we tumbled out of our bunks in the dark protesting at the clamour, dressed and slowly gathered on the parade ground outside under the blaze of searchlights.

There we waited for hours. Dawn broke over the hills – another beautiful day and we were counted again, and again. While we stood in despondent groups in ranks of five we wondered what had happened.

We feared the worst and slowly it was revealed: the tunnel, most of our secret stores of food, some of our clothes and our maps had been discovered. They had won again, and – we had lost. For the camp it meant defeat – not only for those of us in the escape team, but for the many others who had given months of untiring effort to help us.

But why had the Germans, suddenly, and after so many months, decided to pounce at one o'clock in the morning and tear the camp to near-destruction? For some reason our little *poseur* was taken away to disclose most of the secrets we had nurtured and guarded for six long months. For he proved to be a traitor.

What exactly happened we will never know. David Campbell reported that he had seen him being taken 'through the wire' into the German quarters the previous evening and that he had shouted to Campbell, as he was bundled away, that they had searched him and found a map in his kit and were taking him away for questioning. But why him? As I was in charge of the Mapping Department I knew he was lying. There was no rhyme or reason for such a story. Could he have been planted in our midst all the time or was it because he feared dreadful consequences when we escaped and decided to save himself and get out before it was too late?

He could have had no maps, for everything was carefully collected and hidden after map-making was finished each day.

Anyway he was taken away by the Germans to whom presumably he revealed all. How could it have been otherwise, for when the Germans burst into our side of the camp they went straight to the hidden entrance of the tunnel, to most of the 'hides' behind the walls and under floors where our food, clothing and documents were carefully concealed. As I write of these memories I realise now that he must have spent a great deal of time observing and locating the Escape Committee's secrets.

Why did he do it? Not because he was a soldier – there were a hundred other soldiers of all ranks at Rotenburg, but they weren't pretending to be officers. Who cared anyway? But he did. Was it because he was fearful of our awareness of his subterfuge? And the consequences which would befall him after the war – possibly a court martial and imprisonment for posing as an officer? In the First World War, only twenty-five years earlier, a soldier was shot for less.

What was definitive and irrefutable was the completeness of the betrayal. For it was betrayal by someone – complete and utter betrayal.

He never came back into the camp, and two years later was allegedly found by the Allies, dressed in German uniform. The Army dismissed all the charges levelled against him by hundreds of repatriated officers on the grounds that he was not responsible for his actions – what a joke! A sick joke indeed. The reaction from those tragic hours was the beginning of worse to come.

All that day the Germans swarmed over the camp, and we began to despair as to where and when it would all finish. Having tasted success the Germans were still trigger-happy. The gymnasium and large areas of the camp were sealed off and, as our guards stormed about, we wondered, what next?

One factor mystified them and that was to know where we had hidden the earth and sand we had removed from the tunnel. The engineer officers reckoned that we must have dug out over 30 tons of 'spoil', but the Germans could not find any sign of such quantities of earth. It was, in fact, all hidden in the eaves under the roof of the building. To remove 30 tons of earth from the roof of a solid well-built building was in itself an engineering problem which had them guessing for long after we left the camp. We had lost everything else, except our radio (or 'canary' as we called it) in the discovery of the tunnel, but we felt we had won that point.

It was not until several months later, when other officers arrived at our camp from Oflag IX AH Spangenberg, that we learned that the attempts of a tunnel in that castle camp where I had started life in Germany had also been revealed the night our tunnel was discovered, suggesting once more the presence of a traitor who had also seen the efforts being made there.

Night came and we were allowed to go to bed. I was exhausted and I slept, but when I awoke I realised something dreadful had happened.

The others in our room, 'Sam' Parker, David Campbell, Peter Green minus one leg, Charlie Madden, Jake Bolton, Billy Winnington, the two doctors and Robin Campbell, were sitting up in their bunks silent and in a state of shock. For Brigadier Nicholson had been found dead during the night.

Death is always a shock: but in a prison camp – where most of us had already survived death, or near death, in some form or other – it was closer than most of us cared to discuss.

Claude Nicholson, a substantive brigadier, was then the second most senior officer of the British Army prisoners in captivity in Germany. He was already a national figure at home because of his stand at Calais. He was, until his death, albeit in capture, an officer with a future. But the war was unkind to him. Apart from being sacrificed with his force of Green Jackets at Calais in 1940, he had the problem of our camp's involvement with the massacre at Katyn; and of the growing resentment within the camp that a traitor had been seemingly allowed to continue his deception and had not been sent to a soldiers' camp. Also he was not a strong man and was often taken ill.

The uninitiated must not misunderstand the military hierarchy of those days. It was the Germans who imposed their hierarchy on ours and they did not like anyone who interfered with the military order of our lives, prisoners as well as our guards. Unfortunately, our 'little friend' had played with fire and in so doing endangered himself, and ourselves. And at last he had decided to save his own skin, irrespective of the consequences.

Claude Nicholson was undoubtedly one of the consequences. As a man he had done more for the war effort than our little traitor knew was possible. His death was just another blow in our lives. The doctors were concerned about the morale in the camp and we were discreetly told to watch those who were known to be depressed – more so than the rest of us.

Happily the atmosphere improved – the weather was warm and accommodating and this enabled us to get out of the confines of the prison building, and sit and lie about outside in the sun. But the Brigadier's death put a damper on most activities, and our immediate attention was occupied with preparations for the funeral.

The Germans, strangely formal on such occasions, arranged for the Brigadier's body to be buried with full military honours in the nearby cemetery. We were asked to nominate an officer from each country represented in the camp; Scotland, England, Ireland, Australia, New Zealand, Canada, the United States. There were others too. A Roman Catholic priest, Padre Charlton, who had been with a battalion of my regiment, the Gordon Highlanders, said Mass early on the morning of the funeral in the gymnasium and stood at the entrance and saw to it that every Roman Catholic officer and soldier went to the Mass. There were many others who prayed for the Brigadier's soul.

The turnout of the camp's funeral party was impressive. And so indeed was the German parade – all their officers were present, dressed in their best uniforms. Everyone tried to contribute a piece of uniform or headgear, which had survived captivity or had been sent out from home in Red Cross parcels.

17

I Try Again

I cannot claim to know properly what I was really thinking or doing at that time. I was frustrated, bitterly disappointed about the failure of our escape tunnel and the sacrifice of our food, time and effort; and so I decided to try on my own, in which case I would not have to accede to the decisions of others.

I planned to go through the front gate of the camp. I don't know why no one else there had thought about this possibility, as Antony Imbert-Terry had at Spangenberg. Maybe it was because everything had been concentrated on the big break.

Very simply, I had noticed that every day an old farmer was allowed into the camp to collect the rubbish – edible rubbish, potato peelings, and take this 'gash', as we called it, back to his pigs. He arrived at the camp at midday or thereabouts, dragging a hand-cart behind him. He was allowed through the double barbed-wire gates, past the sentries there and into the camp under the surveillance of the other guards in their sentry-boxes high up in their towers. The old man was dressed in faded blue denims or the equivalent, and he wore a German style cap.

He trundled his way across the parade ground, hauling his cart behind him and keeping out of the way of the hockey players to his left. He then went down a gentle slope to a rear door of the main building which led into the kitchens, and relaxed and chatted to the soldiers working there. The one thing which always distracted his attention was a cigarette. We had plenty of those for we each received fifty a week from the Red Cross, and not all of us smoked. To take advantage of his liking for a surreptitious smoke was not easy, for he was watchful and had a countryman's alertness. If he had been found out the Germans would have been quite ruthless – probably punished him and not allowed him in the camp again.

If his attention could be momentarily caught my intention was to climb quickly into the cart and get the cookhouse orderlies to cover me with their rubbish and help by pushing the cart out of the kitchens up the small slope on to the parade ground and then, with a final shove, let the farmer haul his rubbish away for his pigs – with me as passenger. After being let through the large double barbed-wire gates – about 10 ft or more apart – he turned right, down a small path along the outside of the wire in to the road which ran alongside and past the camp back to his holding.

I planned to jump out of the cart somewhere along this road and run off towards the river and into the forest. The whole effort depended on speed and on the fact that the farmer was old and would not be able to do much except raise the alarm. The woods were not far away and by using the river I hoped to break my scent from the dogs when the Germans came after me.

Somehow my French uniform had escaped detection; a French soldier's khaki jacket, my breeches and puttees were still the ones I had been given in Rennes, and I was still wearing my French boots. I also had a rucksack and I was given food from our meagre supplies. Geoffrey MacNab also gave me some maps. The rest was up to me.

I practised the routine for several days. I ate my lunch quickly – I always attended the first of the two sittings – and then made my way down to the kitchens and hung about, noting when the old man arrived, what his every movement was and how much room there would be for me in the cart, and how much of the potato peelings would be needed to cover me properly so that there were none left over to alert the suspicions of the farmer. While the orderlies kept the old man talking I tried the cart for size a few times. The soldiers could speak a smattering of German – some very well – so language was no problem.

Only a very few people knew of my plan: the Escape Committee, most of whom were in my mess anyway; David, and Gerard Brett who was to have escaped with me through the tunnel. I would have preferred to have had them go with me, but there was only one cart and it was only allowed into the camp once a day. So, scared though I was, it was the only way. At that time no other scheme had been approved although the ingenuity of other prisoners was already working up other attempts.

The day I chose for my escape was fine, hot and with little breeze. It was going to be stifling under those potato skins. I was very jumpy all that morning, and I prayed to myself quite often. Lunchtime came. I did not eat much and my companions in the mess said little or nothing – there was nothing to say anyway.

Luncheon seemed never-ending, but eventually people finished their soup and began to wander away to sleep or to their books, making way for the second sitting of 'soup' which would follow. Without even saying goodbye I left my table and slipped away down the stairs to the kitchens. There I was met by David with my French army jacket and rucksack and I hastily finished dressing and waited.

Right on time the old farmer arrived, and as he hauled his cart into the kitchens he made his usual grunted 'Morgen'. While the orderlies engaged him in conversation and offered him a cigarette, he turned his back to get a light and said, 'Haben sie Feuer?' Quickly I was in the cart, lying on my left side, and just as quickly had a dustbin of potato peelings – then another – and then another – tipped over me.

Geoff MacNab had asked me how I was to breathe and not suffocate, and I told him that I would be able to breathe through the gaps between the side-planks of the cart. Strange, but the Germans then – and still – build their country carts – both the big ones drawn by oxen, and the smaller hand-carts like the one in which I was hiding – with sloping sides, and the old cart had plenty of air-space between the slats through which I could breathe. But it was hot, and I doubt if I could have taken very much had there been any delay.

There was no delay. Once the illicit cigarette was finished, the old man grunted his 'Auf Wiedersehens' and 'Dankes' and started to pull the cart out into the courtyard. With a casual, but

determined, push from a couple of soldiers, he pulled the cart
up the slope and then slowly across the yard to the gates.

I could not believe that I was actually going to be pulled out of
the camp to freedom. With more grunts the old man stopped at
the first gates and waited while the Germans unlocked them –
then with a jerk he pulled the cart slowly across the gap between
the high wire fence to the next set of gates and waited while a
guard opened those before hauling the cart out of the camp
'wire' and on to the perimeter path.

Then. One of the guard-dogs, not normally there during the
day, came up and proceeded to cock his leg in the approved
manner on the cart – I could hear him. He then started sniffing
into the potato peelings; then, still sniffing, he started whining.
The dog must have alerted the old man for suddenly I heard him
grunt some words and then felt a hand digging down into the
peelings and fumbling at my right shoulder. He shouted and I
realised that the game was up. For a few seconds I lay very still,
but as the shouting grew nearer and I could hear the sound of
running feet I decided I had best give up. With a heave I
surfaced.

I had potato peelings sticking out of my hair, my mouth and
my ears, my face was burning hot from the heat of the cart, I was
sweating, and I was immediately very still, for looking down at
me and fumbling at his revolver holster for his big Luger pistol
was the camp Sergeant-Major, funnily enough looking just as
apprehensive and nervous as I was. The next few moments were
tense – the dog was barking, the old man was swearing – more
concerned with his pig-swill than with me – the Feldwebel was
shouting at some soldiers and they, who like all good German
soldiers were doing their best to show their readiness for the
next order, were shouting 'Jawohl, jawohl!' I sat there in the
cart for several minutes, not daring to move, waiting until
things quietened down – and then almost courteously I was
hauled upright and out of the cart.

There was little reaction from those inside the camp, either
out of fear for me and what might happen to me next or to them

even, and the people inside kept their distance, that is except David who had been monitoring my movements – David who was always looking for a fight and was fearless. The sentries were by now very alert and there was a great deal of shouting between them.

Also it was still lunch-time for the second sitting, and many of the first sitting were already busy with their after luncheon naps or 'blanket pressing' as we called it. So there were not many people about. Eventually the guards quietened down and completed my exit for me. Leading me out through the outer wire and pushing me in front of them they hustled me along outside the wire down on to the road, and along the road in front of the camp, and the parade ground to the front of the building and into the 'German side' of the camp. Meanwhile David was keeping pace with us, but from inside the camp wire despite the shouts from my escort to him to go away – eventually we left him behind as I was pushed into the German Kommandantur and was alone with the Germans.

I was escorted through the front door of the building as it were, and into some offices. I felt foolish and apprehensive. But their reaction was not particularly hostile. On the contrary the atmosphere was comparatively relaxed, and they seemed pleased that they had caught me so easily. Other escapers in similar circumstances had been roughly treated.

I was searched down to the skin – that was routine – then the camp security officer, Hauptmann Heyl, arrived and started to question me. 'You are very stupid. Why do you try to escape?'

I shrugged my shoulders and did not reply.

'You would not get far,' he said, 'and it is very dangerous.' I looked at him – he was quite relaxed, almost accommodatingly so. 'Yes – very dangerous, for you would surely have been caught and probably shot by the Gestapo – you know what they are like.' I looked at him, but he was deadly serious. Mention of the Gestapo made even the speaker look suddenly apprehensive. 'Gestapo' (short for Geheime Staatspolizei), perhaps more than any other word, expressed the horror of those days.

Seeing the concern on my face he went on to tell me that I
was known by the Germans to be a Commando and then he
reminded me of the Führer's recent orders issued by the OKW
– Oberkommando der Wehrmacht – to the effect that if 'individual persons belonging to Commando Units came into the
hands of the German armed forces then they must be immediately handed over to the SS and that any safe-keeping under
Military protection, i.e. POW camps, even if unintentional,
was strictly forbidden.' In other words should I have been
captured during my escape there would have been very little
hope of being returned to a POW camp. The order, issued
under the direct name of 'Der Führer', was dated 18 October
1942 – the year before – Number 003830/42 S. Kdos OKW, den
18.10.1942; and the extracts that follow are a literal translation
from the original German:

> For a long time now our enemies have used war methods which
> are outside the international Geneva Conventions. These men
> belonging to the so-called Commandos behave in an especially
> brutal and underhand manner and they themselves, as has been
> confirmed, are partially recruited from the ranks of criminals
> set free in the enemy countries. From orders which we have
> managed to capture, it seems that they are authorised not only to
> capture prisoners but to kill even unarmed prisoners without
> hesitation as soon as they believe that they might, in pursuance
> of their aims, represent a burden as prisoners or might be an
> encumbrance. Finally, orders have been found in which the
> killing of prisoners has been required in principle.

It continues as follows:

> For this reason it has already been notified, in addition to the
> communiqué of the High Command of 7.10.1942, that in the
> future Germany would fight against these sabotage troops of the
> British and their allies in the same manner, i.e.: they will be
> exterminated in battle by German troops regardless, wherever
> they are found.

As a result of this Order Commando officers and other ranks captured later in 1942, the year of the order, during the raid on Bordeaux – described by Brigadier Lucas Phillips in his book *Cockleshell Heroes* – were mostly shot when they were captured. And another group of Commandos captured in Norway during their efforts to destroy a German heavy water plant were also executed on capture. So the order was operative, although dependent on the circumstances of capture or recapture.

Hitler's orders applied not only to Commando units, for part of the orders said 'it is of no consequence whether the enemy land for their activities from ships, airplanes or by parachutes. If these subjects when they are discovered seemingly attempt to give themselves up as prisoners, they must be refused any pardon . . .'

Much publicity had since been given to these orders which were brought about by the frustration that the Germans felt about the increasing success of Commando raids. The orders had also been publicised in the German Press and on the German radio at the time. Strangely, they had made little impact on those of us who were Commandos and then in POW camps.

But this reference by Heyl was my first experience of the sinister implications of Hitler's order. Heyl did not say much more except to make a passing reference to the recent rain and unsettled summer weather and more cold to come and how stupid I was.

There was no shouting and after a few more questions he took me by the arm and showed me out of the room into the corridor and, limping with his wooden leg, walked me to the barbed wire barrier which separated the German Kommandantur from the rest of the camp.

Opening the barbed wire gate a sentry then pushed me through into the prison side of Offizierlager IX AZ – I was back 'home', if it could be called that, and I had achieved nothing.

David and the others were waiting for me. There was nothing to say. Another escape route had been exposed, another set of maps lost, and the food which represented several weeks of hard saving – irreplaceable chocolate, oatmeal and sugar – was lost.

Strangely enough, I was not so very depressed. On the contrary, I had tested myself – although failing to succeed. As I had waited, during that lunch before my effort, I had nearly given in to the temptation of not going. To walk 600 miles across Germany and down through France to the Spanish border, alone, was a daunting task and I had not dared to let myself think too much about the prospect.

Next time? If there was to be a next time I would go with a companion. At least I had tried, however, and miserable failure though I had been, I had a certain satisfaction in having attempted to break the bonds of captivity.

When someone tried to escape, the normal procedure on recapture was a spell in the 'cooler' – a punishment cell for the escaper. At Rotenburg 'Micky' Burn had been the last occupant before he was sent on to Colditz.

I was left alone, however. Days went by, and nothing was ever said to me or to the Senior British Officer who, twice a day and every day, met with the German officers as they counted us on 'Appel'. No, nothing was said and it seemed as though the Germans were turning a blind eye to the episode.

18

'Grands Blessés'

Several months earlier an International Red Cross mission had visited the camp and examined those of us who had been recommended by our own doctors for repatriation. Probably – I do not know for certain – that was the reason I had been sent to Ober Masfeld, and then to Rotenburg, to join the other 'Grands Blessés' already passed for repatriation, but still waiting to be repatriated.

The Red Cross delegation – in this case led by a Swiss officer – consisted of a German officer and another Swiss officer, a military doctor in his grey uniform and long cloak. He in turn was accompanied by the local British and German camp doctors. They interviewed us one by one and listened to each individual case. As always in a prison camp there was a mixture of humour and sadness about the proceedings, bitter humour though it may have been.

To be 'passed' as a 'Grand Blessé', a prisoner had to be either seriously wounded, blind, deaf, or ill with cancer, TB, or suffering from a similar serious complaint.

Working on the premise that 'all is fair in love and war' there were a very few cases where the doctors 'accidentally' passed people unfit for further hostilities – because that is what repatriation was all about – but who were to all intents and purposes as fit as could be expected.

There was one officer at Rotenburg who was the acme of smartness and military bearing. He had a magnificent moustache, his hair was always brushed, and he was as upright as a ramrod. But when we received a few days' warning of the Red Cross delegation's next arrival this officer, a major in the regular Army, went to work. Smoking cigarette after cigarette, he somehow kept himself awake without sleep for two nights. He removed his false teeth, brushed his moustache down over his mouth and let his magnificent head of hair fall over his ears. The morning the Red Cross Board arrived and started their examinations, the major, more dead than alive, was looking like death, and with a magnificent though ghoulish sense of playacting, he was kindly helped to a chair, examined and, half-fainting with exhaustion and nicotine poisoning, was immediately waved away by the Swiss doctor, fearful that the major would die there and then, as unfit for further military service.

Another case involved a close friend of mine, already partially deaf from Stuka dive-bombing in 1940. By feigning and practising complete deafness he was able to persuade the doctors of his total disability, although this was an old trick that had been tried before. When my friend was examined and questioned he played 'deaf and dumb' with such success that he was told he would be sent home as soon as possible. But he took no notice. After being told again, and again, and finally pushed towards the door, he staggered away out of the medical room. As he did so the German doctor said, 'Good luck, Captain – and mind the step,' but my friend did not even pause or look round, tripped over the step, staggered out of the door and walked blindly away.

Those were exceptions, for most cases were serious, tragic even, and the majority who were passed unfit for further hostilities were genuinely disabled or sick.

My turn came and I limped into the examination room. There the doctors very politely and gently tried to bend my leg, twisted it, and asked my rank and service. 'Ach So, ein Oberleutnant und Infantrie' said the German doctor, 'you will never fight again – you will be sent home – for you the war is finished.'

I could hardly believe my ears, but I dared not register any emotion in case the doctors changed their minds. Politely they pointed to the door, and I limped away, not daring even to thank them.

It was not so, however, for a young RAF fighter pilot who

followed me. He had just been shot down off the coast over the North Sea and had only been a prisoner for a few months. He was also wounded in his leg and was just as stiff-jointed as myself. But when questioned about his service the German doctor said, 'Ah, but Oberst Bader can fly and he has no legs.' Poor Wentworth Beaumont★ – 'Wenty' as he was called – was then refused repatriation.

Repatriation, however, to us was still a meaningless word and as soon as the Red Cross delegation left the camp, life returned to normal. Although we had been served double rations of bread, Tapfel margarine, and black syrup that day, we were on half rations the following day to make up the deficiency created in our rations. The Red Cross had departed – they had said kind words – they had been a small beam of light in the gloom of our lives, but we had little or no faith in their promises. The Rouen fiasco and failure of the first attempt at repatriation in 1941 was too recent a memory for the older prisoners in the camp, and they would never trust our captors. We, the new prisoners, now officially described as 'Grands Blessés', could only hide our hopes and optimism in the faces of those who, three years after the abortive attempt at exchange, at Rouen, were still waiting.

So the tunnel had failed, my own pathetic attempt at escape had come to nothing and the only good thing about those days was improvement in the weather. The sun shone high in the heavens – and we sunbathed, we browsed in the library, we played cricket and softball and enjoyed 'parole walks' along the banks of the Fulda as it meandered its way north to the Weser and thence to the Baltic.

There was a cruel reason for the failure of the first repatriation exchange at Rouen in 1941. Although agreement had been reached with the Germans, and hospital trains from all over Europe had converged on Rouen for their occupants to be shipped back to the United Kingdom, Hitler cancelled the

★ Now Lord Allendale, a distinguished member of The Turf and an ex-Steward of the Jockey Club.

agreement because we did not then have as many German POWs as were held by the Germans following our heavy defeats in France, Belgium and Norway. Breaking every rule of the Geneva Convention, he was demanding an eye for an eye, and it was not until 1943, after the British had captured hundreds of thousands of the enemy in North Africa, that Hitler changed his mind.

For there was another sinister reason behind his logic: in Russia where the great battles were raging to and fro the Germans were being badly mauled and little quarter was being given, particularly by the Russians. Prisoners were given short shrift, even those who were wounded. In many cases no prisoners were taken; the men were shot, including their doctors. So serious was the shortage of doctors, particularly after our victories in North Africa, that Hitler at last agreed to conform with Geneva and the letter of international war and permit an exchange of wounded prisoners *and* the doctors held prisoner by both sides.

Parole walks had been a new development. They were entirely dependent on the trust demanded of us – that of giving our word not to try and escape whilst on a walk. But we refused not to continue to try to escape when not on parole and back in camp.

After nearly two years of captivity in wartime Europe including three prison hospitals, two prisoner-of-war camps and hundreds of miles of seemingly pointless movement by train under the close surveillance of our guards, I was beginning to qualify as an 'old lag' of some experience. With little to show for such frustration and loss of freedom, what effect had this on my attitude to life at that time? In the words of my old friend David Campbell: 'We had to live together' and in so doing many friends emerged from the contacts made in those prison camps so many years ago. The earlier prisoners who had been captured at Dunkirk and St Valéry had, by the time we were caught in 1942, developed 'a little world of their own'. And whilst we were helped by them in the first days of our captivity we were very conscious of being 'new boys'. In many cases we were regarded with a certain amount of suspicion and resentment, but we soon settled down and became ourselves members of that 'little world'.

This life was far removed from life at home, the most unpleasant aspect of which was the continuing lack of food – Red Cross parcels included. For however good they were, we were always short of proper and adequate rations.

It was the lack of calorific content in our rations which presumably accounted for our negative – or almost negative – attitude to women and lack of desire for female company at that time. Desire was there – but as time passed it faded to mere memories and ceased to be of much concern with the exception of the despair and misery inflicted on some of those prisoners whose women could not bear their loneliness and had deserted their men for those lucky enough to be still stationed at home in Britain.

There were many cases of infidelity among the womenfolk of the thousands of us in captivity. One of the worst examples was that of a soldier-prisoner, then in Oflag IX AZ Rotenburg, who received a letter from his wife with the shattering information that she had decided to leave him for another soldier – a foreign soldier, with a difference, for he was 'a soldier in the new modern army then being trained in Britain – not a member of the old white feather army of 1940'! What could we say to comfort him – what could we do to help him face his bleak and lonely future? 'White feather' army indeed – including, we supposed, the ninety men of the Royal Norfolk Regiment who were rounded up into a barn during the fighting before Dunkirk and then grenaded to death – or including those gallant members of the Green Jacket Regiments who fought at Calais for ten days against the X Panzer Division to help save the evacuation of the BEF from the beaches at Bray Dunes, north of Dunkirk.

Concerning infidelity, the Germans had a strict rule for their own unfaithful wives who were caught sleeping with foreign troops – they shot them.

On the subject of morals and our morale I will always remember the young Polish woman – herself a prisoner – who was working in the fields outside the camp at Rotenburg picking up potatoes. She was comely with a typical high-cheeked Slav look about her. She was handsome indeed – and she knew it. And she also knew that she was the focal point of over 535 pairs of male eyes. She was not allowed near enough to our wire cage to speak – we would have made her understand all right – but she seemed to delight in attracting our attention and we liked looking at her – but there our romance ended.

She and the young French girls at Rennes were as near as I was ever able to get to a woman to test my reactions.

With exceptions, this was true for most of us and in the background there was that fearful punishment the Germans would inflict on their women if we were able to get at them. 'In that world of our own' we took each day as it came, some using the time to good effect with music, painting and some, as always, trying to escape.*

One ex-POW stated how difficult it was to explain that life – there was no way of comparing it with life at home. Another in the same context pointed out how false an impression had been created by the TV series about Colditz – in his words 'an impression out of all proportion to the realities of prison life' – the monotony, the wire, and as always, the lack of food.

The extension of parole and the ability to walk through the surrounding countryside of the beautiful Fulda Valley was pleasant enough but was of little significance in our lives. Rather we took it as a gesture of relaxation by the Germans now that the war was going against them and more and more in our favour.

In recent months we had seen the increasing waves of American bombers who were flying over us and bombing deep into the heart of Germany by day, albeit with heavy casualties, and

* A 1981 BBC Radio 4 programme arranged by David Wade on the subject of the life of POWs brought that life into powerful focus as he recorded the voices of those who were prisoners in Europe and particularly Germany.

on three separate occasions at night on the nearby city of Kassel where the RAF virtually destroyed the city with raids of over 2000 RAF bombers each time.

There was increased movement with new prisoners coming into the camp, including airmen who had been shot down on recent raids and, more significantly, prisoners who were being brought into Germany away from the advancing columns of the 5th Army and 8th Army then advancing north through Italy – the Italian forces having by then collapsed. There was a feeling of excitement in the air.

Suddenly, without warning, a hundred or so officers who had been earmarked for repatriation were told that they would be going home within the next few days and that they were to get ready to leave. The only officer who had been earmarked for repatriation but who was not warned for departure was myself. No reason was given – whilst people were friendly and sympathetic it looked to me as if I was after all going to be punished for my attempted escape. Or worse, that I was to be moved elsewhere in accordance with Hitler's orders.

I regret to say that my emotions were far from controlled and I was very near to violent reaction on that last day of captivity for those earmarked to go home. Admittedly there were hundreds of other officers still to be left behind in the camp, but they had either not been wounded or were not yet passed for repatriation. Then, suddenly, late that afternoon, I was sent for and told that I was to be sent home provided that I did not try any further stupid efforts to escape.

And so, later that evening, on 17 October 1943, a hundred or so officers were marched out of the camp gates through which I had recently tried to escape and down the country lane to the marshalling yards of the nearby railway station. Night fell and the Germans allowed us to wander freely until a train slowly shunted into the station and moved off north-eastward with us its passengers, guarded by a minimum of sentries.

It is difficult to describe how one felt after two years of captivity, and when early the next morning we rattled slowly through the outskirts of the West End of Berlin, we could not yet accept that freedom lay ahead. From Berlin we travelled slowly north and finally reached the Baltic coast at Sassnitz. Here we once more were shunted through some marshalling yards and eventually came to a halt, descended on to the station yard and were allowed to walk along the dockside looking across the grey cold waters of the Baltic. We still did not believe it possible that we were being released, but then suddenly a large ferry ship tied up alongside a quay on the waterfront and within a matter of minutes we walked on board – those few of us who could walk. Those who could not were carried on board on stretchers and we moved slowly away from Germany with all its bitter memories of recent years. We still had no idea as to our destination until we arrived at Trelleborg, a Swedish port on the Baltic, from where we were immediately trans-shipped into a long straggling troop train, only this time with no guards to remind us of captivity.

Our escorts were, on the contrary, very pretty and smartly dressed Lota girls, the Swedish equivalent of the British ATS.

There is nothing very remarkable to record on the next part of our journey to Gothenburg, the big Swedish port, except that, as our train steamed slowly northward it passed another train steaming south, full of German servicemen,* all of them wounded, who were being exchanged for us. Strangely enough we felt little resentment and, apart from a perfunctory wave from some of our people, we passed each other as if captivity was of no consequence in our lives any more; but it had been to obtain the exchange for these German servicemen and their doctors that at last we had attained freedom ourselves.

Three thousand officers and men – seriously sick and wounded men of all services including 1200 protected personnel, i.e., doctors, medical orderlies, chaplains and others exclusively concerned with the care of the sick and wounded – were exchanged at that time.

When we reached Gothenburg we who could walk were told to parade on the seafront alongside the hospital ship which was busy loading other prisoners on board, and there we were introduced to the Crown Princess of Sweden who had come to the port to bid us farewell. Seeing the Commando flashes on my shoulder (which had been sent to me in a letter from home), she said, 'Oh, I see you work for my brother. Please give him my best when you see him in London.' Standing stiffly to attention, I replied, 'Yes, Ma'am,' but with no idea to whom she was referring.

It was not until her small party was led on board the hospital ship that a Swedish officer said to me, 'You know who her brother is, of course,' to which I had to admit ignorance. 'Oh, but don't you realise that he is Lord Mountbatten and that she is his sister? One day she will be our Queen.' And so, even there in Sweden, the Commando sign had significance.

19

Remembering the Raid

Hardened as we were to living with legless and armless bodies, and the gentle gropings of the blind, we took scant notice of the hours of time it took to transfer the 3000 'Grands Blessés' from the hospital trains to some large hospital ships including the *Drottingholm*. Nevertheless it was late on in the day when we finally cast off from Swedish soil and slowly moved away from the waving Swedes and the port of Gothenberg towards the open sea.

Dawn next day and we were well clear of the Skagerrak and steaming steadily south-westwards into the North Sea, escorted by – of all vessels – a U-boat. And so I was leaving the continent as I had approached it two years before – in the company of a submarine. Quite what the sinister escort was meant to convey no one knew – except could it be to prove to us that the enemy was still a force to be considered and that we had to be escorted all the way home to safety?

Suddenly, however, the submarine dived beneath the cold grey waters of the North Sea, and a few minutes later the reason why flew towards us from the west – a plane, blunt-looking and camouflaged in the dark green and black of the RAF – a Beaufighter, a heavy, twin-engined fighter more than capable of dealing with a submarine. A brutal reminder that the war was still at 'action stations' for both sides.

A few more miles and an aircraft carrier hove into view, and then other vessels. Some I recognised from two years ago, but there were others of different shapes and sizes which I had never seen before – nor had the others, for none of us, sailor, airman or soldier, had seen the new weaponry crowding around our coasts and air space during the previous two years. What at first I thought was *Ark Royal* – one of the only aircraft-carriers I had seen – was in fact a baby 'Flat Top' – a converted merchant ship stripped of its superstructure and converted into a small aircraft-carrier for convoy work.

As we closed the coastline and more ships hove into view the sailors confirmed our guesswork – we were entering the Firth of Forth where I and the others who went to St Nazaire – most now dead and the others still prisoners back in Germany – had started this whole adventure nearly two years before. Soon we were dropping anchor at Leith, Scotland's ancient link with the Continent – the link upon which the Auld Alliance had grown – where Mary Queen of Scots, and her Four Marys, had returned to lay claim to the throne of Scotland, and Mary's subsequent desperate adventuring began with England's Elizabeth which led to her execution. It was also, of course, just a few miles across the Firth of Forth from Burntisland where the first actual preparation and training for the raid had started in February 1942 under the guidance of Captain 'Bill' Pritchard who, sadly, was killed, never to see the success he had planned.

It is difficult to recall all that happened that day. As 'walking wounded', we were well down the list in priority of disembarkation of the 3000 wounded, blind, disabled, and sick. We were impatient, but the Red Cross were all-caring and kind and made our wait as comfortable as possible with hundreds of cups of tea, made with real fresh milk and unlimited sugar, cigarettes by the thousand and food. But I cannot remember one currant in any one currant bun of that day's rations.

At long last – it was well into the afternoon – it came to our turn to disembark. More welcomes, on shore this time, and there was a band – a bit tired by then but 'blawin' away as if to show their willing best.

And then military discipline slowly took charge – British discipline – a strange and different variant of our recent experience with the Germans. At least there was no shouting – no; had there been one raised voice I believe we would have strangled its owner into oblivion. But discipline there was and we formed up into long lines and repeated our names, ranks, and numbers. Strangely, however, there was no medication – that did not come till we reached our hospitals, scattered all over the country – in our case, for David, Sam, and most of our gang we were directed to a train which rattled its way for hour after hour to the Military Hospital at Netley, near Southampton, 400 miles or more away to the south. Southampton yet again – part of our movement order in 1942.

But home we were. The delay was bearable, but our reception, however, grew less accommodating – some of our reception party must have been getting bored and their drinks and dinner time were drawing nigh. But we could take all they threw at us – this was child's play compared to a German search party; even the irritating and repetitious questioning, aggressive at times, failed to raise our ire. But when a young bespectacled captain – by the tarnish on his pips he could only have been in the Army a year or more – started to question me all over again – *Name*: Chant S.W.; *Rank*: Lieutenant; *Number*: 105159, and in so saying looked at the two frayed and faded pieces of khaki on my shoulders, hesitated, and, looking down at his writing said, 'Why were you captured?' – not 'Where' or 'When', but '*Why* were you captured'. 'Why' indeed. Should I tell him of Colonel Newman's warning on board HMS *Princess Josephine Charlotte* during his final briefing?

No, I walked away and left him to fill in that answer for himself.

Although we had not known it at the time, Lord Mountbatten himself said to Newman: 'I want you to be quite clear that this is not just an ordinary raid; it is an important operation of the war. It is also a very hazardous operation. I am quite confident that you will get in and do the job all right but I don't expect any of you to get out again . . .!'

That this successful action had been achieved at such desperate cost was, in my opinion, owing to two vital factors: the failure of the RAF to identify our target area – the docks – and to bomb and distract and confuse the enemy. This is, of course, no criticism of the RAF, for their standing instructions, ever since Dunkirk, required them not to attack any target unless it could be clearly identified from the air.

The other factor for which the planners must take full responsibility was the failure to supply us with stronger and more powerful naval craft, such as one, or preferably two more old American destroyers (of the original 50 US destroyers which Churchill traded with Roosevelt the majority were still in service in the Royal Navy at that time). These could have been used to transport us, the Commandos, there, and then with-draw us – out to sea to be trans-shipped to our covering, more modern, destroyers.* Taken to its ultimate assessment our MLs were not built to absorb the shellfire of heavy coastal artillery such as 88 mm and 105 mm guns; 20-40 mm guns maybe, but even that was doubtful because of the high octane fuel being used in the ML engines. One shell in the fuel tanks and they caught fire or exploded.

These are the facts as we now know them, although at the time they were not appreciated, so diffuse were the individual actions which took place at St Nazaire and which led those back in Britain to suspect that the raid had failed.

As the years passed, however, the true pattern of events emerged to prove beyond doubt that Operation CHARIOT was one of the most successful Commando raids ever carried out during the Second World War.

Despite the official misgivings about the success of the raid at the time, I knew we had achieved all our major objectives, even though it was at great cost of life.

---

* On 19 March 1942 a vital meeting had discussed this problem. Mountbatten was in the chair and pleaded for two or more destroyers, but the Admiralty said 'No' and instead offered a flotilla of motor launches – Fairmiles of 'our light coastal forces' made of wood and highly inflammable.

EPILOGUE

When I was repatriated from Germany back to Britain at the end of 1943 I was sent on leave and also debriefed at COHQ by a charming and pretty young lady, an ATS captain named Jean Nicholls, and others. Then to my absolute amazement, one Sunday morning, weeks after my arrival in London, the national Press published my account of what had happened during the fighting on land, in the docks of St Nazaire. I realised I was the first officer to return to Britain who had actually landed and fought in the port, and later had met up with the others who survived and were still prisoners in Germany.

A few weeks later I was zigzagging across the Atlantic in the liner, *Mauretania*, bound for a lecture and writing tour of the USA.

I spent several months there and lectured twice and sometimes three times a day to every kind of audience – men's and women's clubs, Rotarians, Lions, uptown and downtown; union gatherings, dockyard workers, Harvard University, Washington University, and schools, not forgetting masses of servicemen of every rank. I travelled from New York and Washington right across to California and to Hollywood; to San Francisco, into Canada and Vancouver; back to Winnipeg, down into the States, Minneapolis, Chicago, Buffalo and finally New York again. I covered some 8000 or 9000 miles – all by train as plane travel was reserved for top priority travellers – and I was no longer top priority.

My mission was part of a belated effort by His Majesty's Government to explain to the Americans that Britain was still fighting in the war and winning – for Errol Flynn and other Hollywood stars were winning the war and John Wayne it was who landed in France on D-Day! It was a memorable experience and I made many friends.

I flew back to Prestwick, Scotland, in a bomber with a group or RAF pilots to find that D-Day was already D+100 or so. After some months I settled in at the War Office as a Major – promotion at last. I served there until the war ended.

There was no place in the peacetime army, then, for a wounded infantry officer and it was quite by chance that I got a job working for the newly established film empire, the Rank Organisation. Then came an exciting if frustrating five years: luckily however I was with the cream, then, of this sometimes highly strung art form. To name a few: David Lean, the director; Noël Coward, 'the master' to everyone in the business; Richard Todd, then young and just starting his climb to stardom; Trevor Howard, star of *Brief Encounter* with his co-star Celia Johnson.

There were others and the films we made at Pinewood – including *Brief Encounter*, *Great Expectations*, *Oliver Twist* – did not hide the difficult stresses and undercurrents of emotion of the film world.

To my utter and complete relief I was telephoned one day by the War Office and asked if I could return to the Army. I asked where I was to go and the reply was, 'I'm sorry to give you so little notice but we want to post you to the new HQ under the command of General Eisenhower in Paris.'

The chance to escape from a world of make-believe back to reality was too great and within days I was in Paris walking every morning to SHAPE HQ. I had to answer to both General Eisenhower (the Supreme Commander of Allied Powers in Europe) and Field Marshal Montgomery, the deputy Supreme Commander. My job was to act as a Liaison Officer, and as a result I met almost every statesman and politician in America and Europe. I was now a Lieutenant-Colonel, had been awarded the OBE (Mil), and I had often acted as ADC to General 'Ike' and, later, to his successors, particularly Generals Ridgway and Gruenther.

My wife by this time had succeeded to her father's title and become The Lady Sempill. A Sempill lady was one of Mary Queen of Scots' 'Four Marys'. In order to 'keep up with the Joneses', as it were, I assumed by decree of Lyon Court in Scotland the name of Sempill – one of Scotland's oldest families, going back to the thirteenth century.

Since those days I have travelled around the world several times representing international companies and organisations. When the Transglobe Expedition was planned I was made Chairman of the Public Relations Committee and through this travelled round the world again.

Not until years later when I discussed those days with a retired major, 'Bill' Ormerod, who was responsible in part for my lecture tour, did I discover that I was one of only twelve officers from all three services selected for this special duty. They included a submariner commander of great fame, fighter pilots and the rest, like myself, were Army officers. After the war those of us who had survived the raid returned to St Nazaire, travelling on board HMS *Sirius* – a light cruiser which was not very comfortable and rather run down; but we did not complain for it was the first-ever chance we had had of meeting again since the night of 28 March 1942.

The French gave us a rousing welcome and we were received by the President of France, M Ramadier. This was the occasion when he said 'You were the first to give us hope!' His Majesty the King was represented by the British Ambassador – then Sir Duff Cooper, later Viscount Norwich. He was accompanied by Lady Diana Cooper.

In 1982, forty years later, it was decided to mark our annual reunion by a return to St Nazaire to honour those who died in the raid. Over 120 sailors and soldiers were traced and plans were being made to transport the party by road and ferry across the Channel and Brittany to the Loire. Then suddenly, to our delight, HRH The Duke of Edinburgh, our patron, was informed by Her Majesty The Queen that we were 'invited by Her Gracious Majesty to travel on board the Royal Yacht *Britannia* from Portsmouth to St Nazaire on Thursday, 22 April 1982.'

What greater honour could have been accorded us – the first ever time that Her Majesty has allowed the Royal Yacht to be used for such an occasion.

At the service held in front of the simple memorial erected by the French after the war near the scene of our fighting the following words were spoken in both French and English:

'Let us remember with gratitude and homage those courageous French men and women who, risking life and liberty, rose spontaneously to our side forty years ago; and those too, from many regions, whose self-denying kindness have given us heart and help on the way to prison or escape. May the friendship between our two countries, formed in arms, be ever strengthened and enriched in peace.

'Let us honour the memory of our Chief, Earl Mountbatten of Burma, to whose audacity, imagination, thoroughness and skill we owe the conception and triumphant planning of our raid.

'Let us remember the fallen. R.I.P.'

APPENDIX 1

Citations for the five VCs awarded for the Raid
ADMIRALTY

Whitehall,
21st May, 1942.

The KING has been graciously pleased to approve the award of the VICTORIA CROSS for daring and valour in the attack on the German Naval Base at St Nazaire, to:–

Commander Robert Edward Dudley RYDER, Royal Navy.

For great gallantry in the attack on St Nazaire. He commanded a force of small unprotected ships in an attack on a heavily defended port and led HMS *Campbeltown* in under intense fire from short range weapons at point blank range. Though the main object of the expedition had been accomplished in the beaching of *Campbeltown*, he remained on the spot conducting operations, evacuating men from *Campbeltown* and dealing with strong points and close range weapons while exposed to heavy fire for one hour and sixteen minutes, and did not withdraw till it was certain that his ship could be of no use in rescuing any of the Commando Troops who were still ashore. That his Motor Gun Boat, now full of dead and wounded, should have survived and should have been able to withdraw through an intense barrage of close range fire was almost a miracle.

Lieutenant-Commander Stephen Halden BEATTIE, Royal Navy, HMS *Campbeltown*.

For great gallantry and determination in the attack on St Nazaire in command of HMS *Campbeltown*. Under intense fire directed at the bridge from point blank range of about 100 yards, and in the face of the blinding glare of many searchlights, he steamed her into the lock-gates and beached and scuttled her in the correct position.

This Victoria Cross is awarded to Lieutenant-Commander Beattie in recognition not only of his own valour but also of that of the unnamed officers and men of a very gallant ship's company, many of whom have not returned.

Able Seaman William Alfred SAVAGE, C/JX. 173910.

For great gallantry, skill and devotion to duty as gunlayer of the pom-pom in a motor gun boat in the St Nazaire raid. Completely exposed, and under heavy fire he engaged positions ashore with cool and steady accuracy. On the way out of the harbour he kept up the same vigorous and accurate fire against the attacking ships, until he was killed at his gun.

This Victoria Cross is awarded in recognition not only of the gallantry and devotion to duty of Able Seaman Savage, but also of the valour shown by many others, unnamed, in Motor Launches, Motor Gun Boats and Motor Torpedo Boats, who gallantly carried out their duty in entirely exposed positions against enemy fire at very close range.

WAR OFFICE

19th June, 1945.

The KING has been graciously pleased to approve the award of the VICTORIA CROSS to:-

Lieutenant-Colonel Augustus Charles NEWMAN (33927), The Essex Regiment (attached Commandos) (Salford, Bucks.).

On the night of 27th/28th March, 1942, Lieutenant-Colonel Newman was in command of the military force detailed to land on enemy occupied territory and destroy the dock installations of the German controlled naval base at St Nazaire.

This important base was known to be heavily defended and bomber support had to be abandoned owing to bad weather. The operation was therefore bound to be exceedingly hazardous, but Lieutenant-Colonel Newman, although empowered to call off the assault at any stage, was determined to carry to a successful conclusion the important task which had been assigned to him.

Coolly and calmly he stood on the bridge of the leading craft, as the small force steamed up the estuary of the River Loire, although the ships had been caught in the enemy searchlights and a murderous crossfire opened from both banks, causing heavy casualties.

Although Lieutenant-Colonel Newman need not have landed himself, he was one of the first ashore and, during the next five hours of bitter fighting, he personally entered several houses and

Appendix I

shot up the occupants and supervised the operations in the town, utterly regardless of his own safety, and he never wavered in his resolution to carry through the operation upon which so much depended.

An enemy gun position on the roof of a U-boat pen had been causing heavy casualties to the landing craft and Lieutenant-Colonel Newman directed the fire of a mortar against this position to such effect that the gun was silenced. Still fully exposed, he then brought machine gun fire to bear on an armed trawler in the harbour, compelling it to withdraw and thus preventing many casualties in the main demolition area.

Under the brilliant leadership of this officer the troops fought magnificently and held vastly superior enemy forces at bay, until the demolition parties had successfully completed their work of destruction.

By this time, however, most of the landing craft had been sunk or set on fire and evacuation by sea was no longer possible. Although the main objective had been achieved, Lieutenant-Colonel Newman nevertheless was now determined to try and fight his way out into open country and so give all survivors a chance to escape.

The only way out of the harbour area lay across a narrow iron bridge covered by enemy machine guns and although severely shaken by a German hand grenade, which had burst at his feet, Lieutenant-Colonel Newman personally led the charge which stormed the position and under his inspiring leadership the small force fought its way through the streets to a point near the open country, when, all ammunition expended, he and his men were finally overpowered by the enemy.

The outstanding gallantry and devotion to duty of this fearless officer, his brilliant leadership and initiative, were largely responsible for the success of this perilous operation which resulted in heavy damage to the important naval base at St Nazaire.

WAR OFFICE

19th June, 1945.

The KING has been graciously pleased to approve the posthumous award of the VICTORIA CROSS to:-

No. 18747047 Sergeant Thomas Frank DURRANT, Corps of Royal

Engineers (attached Commandos) (Green Street Green, Farnborough, Kent).

For great gallantry, skill and devotion to duty when in charge of a Lewis gun in H.M. Motor Launch 306 in the St Nazaire raid on the 28th March 1942.

Motor Launch 306 came under heavy fire while proceeding up the River Loire towards the port. Sergeant Durrant, in his position abaft the bridge, where he had no cover or protection, engaged enemy gun positions and searchlights on shore. During this engagement he was severely wounded in the arm but refused to leave his gun.

The Motor Launch subsequently went down the river and was attacked by a German destroyer at 50-60 yards range, and often closer. In this action Sergeant Durrant continued to fire at the destroyer's bridge with the greatest coolness and with complete disregard of the enemy's fire. The Motor Launch was illuminated by the enemy searchlight and Sergeant Durrant drew on himself the individual attention of the enemy guns, and was again wounded, in many places. Despite these further wounds he stayed in his exposed position, still firing his gun, although after a time only able to support himself by holding on to the gun mounting.

After a running fight, the Commander of the German destroyer called on the Motor Launch to surrender. Sergeant Durrant's answer was a further burst of fire at the destroyer's bridge. Although now very weak he went on firing, using drums of ammunition as fast as they could be replaced. A renewed attack by the enemy vessel eventually silenced the fire of the Motor Launch but Sergeant Durrant refused to give up until the destroyer came alongside, grappled the Motor Launch and took prisoner those who remained alive.

Sergeant Durrant's gallant fight was commended by the German officers on boarding the Motor Launch.

This very gallant Non-Commissioned Officer later died of many wounds received in action.

APPENDIX 2

Statistics of Spring Tides and Darkness at St Nazaire

(All times are British Summer Time)

Date	Times between which height of tide is 14 feet	Time of H.W.	Ht.	Sun-rise	Sun-set
28th March	0100–0300	0151	14'	0648	1923
29th March	0130–0345	0231	15' 1"	0647	1925
30th March	0145–0445	0304	16' 4"	0646	1926
31st March	0225–0550	0356	17' 1"	0643	1927
1st April	0250–0635	0430	17' 1"	0640	1938

APPENDIX 3

Naval Personnel Taking Part in Operation CHARIOT

HMS *Campbeltown*

Lieutenant-Commander S. H. Beattie, RN
Lieutenant C. H. Gough, RN
Lieutenant N. T. B. Tibbets, RN
Warrant Engineer W. H. Locke, RN
Gunner (T.) H. Hargreaves, RN
Surgeon-Lieutenant W. J. Winthorpe, RCNVR

A. Love	PO Std		A. T. Bott	O/Sea
A. R. Gooch	L/Std		W. Findley	AB
A. Salter	Std		J. Crook	AB
T. R. Bryant	O/Cook		V. Howard	AB
A. Wellsted	CPO		D. Garlick	AB
D. G. Stanford	Yeo		R. Ferguson	AB
W. Stocker	PO		A. H. Jones	Tel
F. Wherrell	OA		J. Smith	AB
H. Scott	PO Tel		F. Hutchin	AB
W. Newman	PO		J. Demmelweet	AB
H. Booth	PO		D. White	AB
E. Bennett	AB		R. Bailey	L/Sea
A. Paton	AB		H. Howard	CERA
T. Findlay	AB		H. J. Reay	ERA
A. Rollin	AB		R. R. Nelson	ERA
L. Kemp	L/Sea		D.C. Pyke	SPO
B. V. Nelthorpe	O/Sea		R. J. C. Hodder	SPO
D. C. Clark	AB		R. F. Underhill	SPO
E. Davidge	O/Sea		J. W. Purver	SPO
E. Mawby	L/Sea		J. B. Reville	L/Sto
S. Giles	AB		C. W. Baxter	L/Sto
A. Baker	AB		A. T. Wade	SPO
A. Westwell	O/Sig		E. A. Pitt	SPO
R. Teeling	Sig		W. C. Brenton	L/Sto
N. Robinson	Tel		D. E. Turner	L/Sto
H. Wood	AB		J. Mennell	L/Sto
D. Bowman	AB		F. E. Pritchard	L/Sto
J. Millar	AB		W. H. Berry	L/Sto
H. E. Nelson	AB		D. M. Vyall	Sto
A. Ross	O/Sea		R. G. Hancock	Sto

L. J. Newbold	Sto		J. S. Cutter	Sto
A. Dawn	Sto		P. G. Mayes	Sto
R. Richards	Sto		H. A. Stevens	Sto
J. Venture	Sto		W. E. Rainbird	Cook
B. Barnes	Sto			

MGB 314

Commander R. E. D. Ryder, RN Naval Force Commander.
Lieutenant A. R. Green, RN Navigating Officer.
Sub-Lieutenant J. E. O'Rourke, RCNVR Signals Officer.
Ldg. Signalman Pike

Lieutenant D. M. C. Curtis, RNVR
Sub-Lieutenant W. G. L. Brooker, RNVR
Sub-Lieutenant R. T. C. Worsley, RNVR

F. McKee	A/Ldg Sea		A. Sadler	AB
F. S. Hemming	PO MM		H. A. Boswell	O/Sea
R. W. Bannister	A/Ldg Sto		J. E. Cutts	O/Sea
W. Clark	Sto (I)		P. C. Ellingham	O/Sea
G. A. Lang	Sto (I)		C. A. Young	AB
C. E. Whittle	O/Sea		F. A. Smith	AB
A. R. Vallance	O/Sea		A. R. Stephens	AB
W. A. Savage	AB		E. J. Hughes	O/Tel
W. Reynolds	O/Tel			

MTB 74

Sub-Lieutenant R. C. M. V. Wynn, RNVR
Sub-Lieutenant A. F. O'Connor, RNVR

R. R. Ward	PO		C. W. Liddell	AB
W. H. Lovegrove	CMM		D. Bowyer	Tel
E. Hargreaves	AB		H. Simmonds	Ldg/Sto
L. Denison	AB		A. W. Savage	Sto (I)

ML 156

Lieutenant L. Fenton, RNVR
Sub-Lieutenant N. G. Machin, RNVR

T. A. Moyes	A/PO		H. Morgan	AB
P. Reeves	AB		R. Cowling	Tel
I. Doig	AB		C. Hetherell	MM
J. Kennedy	AB		W. J. Thompson	L/Sto
F. Marshall	AB		B. Whittaker	Sto/T

ML 160

Lieutenant T. W. Boyd, RNVR
Sub-Lieutenant J. A. Tait, RNVR
Sub-Lieutentant J. G. Hall, RANVR

L. S. Lamb	A/PO	J. Glass	AB
C. D. Walker	PO	E. A. Edwards	AB
A. J. Rice	A/SPO	R. E. Jones	AB
A. MacIver	A/Ldg Sea	J. Oliphant	St
S. E. Drew	Tel	F. C. Morris	LMM
C. J. Tolley	AB		

ML 177

Sub-Lieutenant M. F. Rodier, RNVR
Sub-Lieutentant W. J. Heaven, RNVR
Sub-Lieutentant (E.) A. J. Toy, RNVR
Acting Sub-Lieutenant F. W. M. Arkell, RNVR

J. Rafferty	PO MM	R. Mitchell	AB
K. Pitt	A/Ldg Sea	J. H. Worth	Sto (I)
J. Brown	AB	E. Jetson	Sto (II)
R. Heeley	Tel	C. H. Miller	AB
H. Dexter	Sto (I)	H. N. Irvin	LMM
R. Rushworth	AB	J. Hextall	O/Sea

ML 192

Lieutenant-Commander W. L. Stephens, RNVR
Sub-Lieutenant S. P. Haighton, RNVR
Sub-Lieutenant R. E. Collinson, RNVR

H. McPhail Bruce	A/PO	G. C. Davidson	O/Tel
G. H. Hallet	O/Sea	S. Davidson	AB
T. G. Burd	AB	G. Snowball	MM
W. E. Farmer	Ldg Sto	J. Hogg Laurie	Ldg Tel
G. Lapsley	AB	M. Corran	AB
H. W. Little	O/Sea	F. G. Chapman	Sto (II)
A. E. Hale	O/Sig	C. S. Aston	MM

ML 262

Lieutenant E. A. Burt, RNVR
Sub-Lieutenant E. C. A. Roberts, RNVR
Sub-Lieutenant K. I. Hills, RNVR

R. Gough	PO MM	G. J. Pryde	Ldg MM
W. E. Leaney	Ldg Sea	F. Sutherland	AB
S. McKeown	Ldg Sea	W. J. Martin	AB

J. D. Walker	AB		C. L. Jones	Sto (II)
F. Hollands	Sto (I)		T. Hudson	AB
L. Ball	Sto (I)		J. A Smith	Tel
G. J. Jones	AB			

ML 267

Lieutenant E. H. Beart, RNVR
Sub-Lieutenant D. Lloyd-Davies, RCNVR
Sub-Lieutenant W. Pirie-Mewes, RNVR

J. H. Gleeson	Ldg Sea		W. Oliphant	Sto (I)
E. Chick	Ldg Sto		A. Sheppard	AB
E. E. Kenningham	Ldg MM		G. Bell	O/Sea
S. W. Roots	PO MM		A. Bartlett	O/Sea
J. Leach	AB		D. M. Steele	O/Tel
R. W. Marshall	AB		H. Westcott	O/Sea
T. Newlands	Sto (I)			

ML 268

Lieutenant A. D. B. Tillie, RNVR
Sub-Lieutenant K. Bachelor, RNVR
Sub-Lieutenant D. Garnham, RNVR

J. M. Younger	Ldg Sto		W. L. Gammage	Tel (I)
J. H. Castle	Ldg Sea		J. Smith	AB
A. Howard	PO MM		J. W. Nicholson	AB
H. Knight	Sto (I)		W. M. Kerr	O/Sea
K. C. Kirkup	Ldg Sea		M. Rakusen	Ldg Sea
S. W. Rivett	Ldg Sea		L. H. Wallace	PO MM

ML 270

Lieutenant C. S. B. Irwin, RNVR
Lieutenant C. W. Wallach, RANVR
Sub-Lieutenant G. V. Fisher, RNZNVR

V. W. H. Adams	PO		J. Elliott	AB
T. Gardener	MM		H. McIntire	O/Sea
F. Axford	L/Tel		L. Holloway	Sto (I)
F. Catton	L/Sea		A. Porter	Sto (I)
W. Turner	AB		L. Kelley	Sig
F. Earl	AB		C. Burkinshor	O/Tel
W. Evans	AB		F. Brown	Sto (II)

ML 298

Sub-Lieutenant N. R. Nock, RNVR
Sub-Lieutenant A. Spraggon, RNVR
Sub-Lieutenant P. Varden-Patten, RNVR

R. Hambley	PO	D. Clear	O/Sea
R. Ramsey	CMM	T. Milner	O/Sea
G. Swann	O/Sea	L. Barber	O/Sea
R. Kirk	O/Tel	E. Dodd	AB
L. C. Smith	Sto (II)	A. Milner	AB
J. R. Mathers	Sto (I)	E. Marsden	CMM
H. A. Wood	AB		

ML 306

Lieutenant I. B. Henderson, RNVR
Sub-Lieutenant P. J. C. Dark, RNVR
Sub-Lieutenant P. W. Landy, RANVR

W. G. Sargent	Ldg Sea	T. N. Garner	O/Sea
A. L. Bennett	PO MM	R. Batteson	O/Sea
W. K. Sparkes	AB	E. A. Butcher	Sto (II)
A. V. Alder	AB	A. Ritchie	Sto (II)
R. H. Newman	Tel	A. Shephard	O/Sea
G. Rees	O/Sea		

ML 307

Lieutenant N. B. Wallis, RANVR
Sub-Lieutenant –.Williamson, RNVR
Sub-Lieutenant L. Clegg, RNVR

P. P. Warrick	Ldg Sea	M. T. Macrae	MM
G. H. Allen	Sto (I)	T. G. Jones	Ldg Sto
B. K. Croft	O/Sea	J. S. Roberts	O/Sea
P.W.J. Woodward	O/Sea	P. S. T. G. Barry	O/Tel
W. Jameson	O/Sea	B. J. Butterworth	AB
R. Manson	O/Sea		

ML 341

Lieutenant D. L. Briault, RNVR
Sub-Lieutenant P. S. Hutchinson, RNZNVR
Sub-Lieutenant A. S. Leggat, RNVR

C. F. Sporrier	Ldg Sea	J. W. Lockwood	O/Sea
J. H. Harpin	Ldg MM	A. Colvin	Sto (II)
A. E. Morgan	Ldg Sto	F. East	O/Sea
E. I. Loweth	O/Tel	H. Bossward	O/Sea

N. Moon	O/Sea	C. T. Piggott	PO MM
W. Thorpe	O/Sea	E. S. McLuckie	Sea RNR

ML 443

Lieutenant K. Horlock, RNVR
Sub-Lieutenant P. Royal, RNVR
Lieutenant E. E. M. Shields, RNVR
Lieutenant R. E. A. Verity, RNVR, Beach Master

W. Hay	Ldg Sto	A. J. Slater	Tel
H. Bracewell	MM	H. Allen	Sto (II)
H. J. Smith	Ldg Sea	R. Biebuyck	Sto (II)
P. J. Brady	Ldg Sea	W. F. E. Gattenby	O/Sea
C. Stone	AB	S. H.	
S. Clayton	O/Sea	Shufflebotham	O/Sea
S. Hayhurst	O/Tel	G. Rowlin	O/Sea
R. G. Lake	O/Tel	F. Folkard	O/Sea

ML 446

Lieutenant H. G. R. Falconar, RNVR
Sub-Lieutenant J. A. May, RNVR
Sub-Lieutenant H. W. Arnold, RNVR

S. H. Elder	W. Watt
J. Ross	T. Butcher
J. L. Hall	W. Wilson
F. Graham	F. Ormiston
T. O'Leary	W. A. Carr
H. Hagart	A. W. Tew

ML 447

Lieutenant T. D. L. Platt, RNR
Lieutenant H. S. Chambers, RNVR
Lieutenant G. MacNaughton Baker, RCNVR

F. Overton	Ldg Sea	T. G. Parker	MM
A. Parsons	Ldg Tel	D. Broome	Sto (I)
H. Drapper	AB	E. Liddicoat	Sto (II)
J. Barrett	AB	A. E. Cotter	
A. C. D. Gordon	AB	J. E. Terrey	Ldg Sea
A. Duncan	O/Sea	D. N. Lambert	AB

ML 457

Lieutenant T. A. M. Collier, RNVR
Sub-Lieutenant K. G. Hampshire, RNVR
Sub-Lieutenant G. E. A. Barham, RNVR

S. J. Onsorge	Ldg Sea	A. H. Jones	O/Tel
J. G. Welch	CMM	L. S. Dickson	O/Sea
P. Mooney	MM	H. V. Phillimore	O/Sea
G. Brearley	AB	L. Outtrim	O/Sea
H. R. Dyer	AB	E. Barber	Sto (II)
J. Parsons	AB	S. Harrison	Sto (II)

MILITARY PERSONNEL

OFFICERS

Lieut-Colonel A. C. Newman	Military Force Commander
Major W. O. Copeland	No 2 Commmando
Captain S. A. Day	No 2 "
Captain M. Barling, RAMC	No 2 "
Captain D. Paton, RAMC	No 2 "
Captain R. Hodgson	No 2 "
Captain D. Birney	No 2 "
Captain R. H. Hooper	No 2 "
Captain D. Roy	No 2 "
Captain M. C. Burn	No 2 "
Lieutenant W. C. Clibborn	No 2 "
Lieutenant M. C. Denison	No 2 "
Lieutenant J. Vanderwerve	No 2 "
Lieutenant J. D. Proctor	No 2 "
Lieutenant J. B. Houghton	No 2 "
Lieutenant J. Roderick	No 2 "
Lieutenant T. G. Peyton	No 2 "
Lieutenant H. H. G. Hopwood	No 2 "
Lieutenant R. F. Morgan	No 2 "
Lieutenant M. Jenkins	No 2 "
2nd Lieutenant J. Stutchbury	No 2 "
2nd Lieutenant W. H. Watson	No 2 "
Lieutenant N. Oughtred	No 2 "
Captain W. H. Pritchard	Special Service Brigade
Lieutenant R. O. C. Swayne	No 1 Commando
Lieutenant P. Walton	No 2 "
Lieutenant W. W. Etches	No 3 "
Captain E. W. Bradley	No 3 "
Lieutenant M. Woodcock	No 3 "
2nd Lieutenant H. Pennington	No 4 "
Lieutenant R. J. Burtinshaw	No 5 "

Lieutenant S. W. Chant	No 5 Commando
Lieutenant G. J. Smalley	No 5 "
Lieutenant J. A. Bonvin	No 6 "
Lieutenant A. D. Wilson	No 9 "
Lieutenant G. Brett	No 12 "
2nd Lieutenant P. Basset-Wilson	No 12 "
Lieutenant C. W. B. Purdon	No 12 "
Captain P. K. Montgomery	Special Service Brigade
Captain D. R. de Jonghe	French
2nd Lieutenant W. G. Lee	French
Captain A. F. A. I. Terry	(Intelligence)
Mr J. M. G. Holman	London *Evening Standard*
Mr E. J. Gilling	Exchange Telegraph

OTHER RANKS

No. 2 COMMANDO
Headquarters :

A. Moss	RSM
A. Seaton	RQMS
G. Taylor	Sgt
D. Steele	Sgt
R. Crippin	Cpl
A. Simister	Cpl
J. Harrington	L/Cpl
T. Hannon	Pte
F. Kelly	Pte
J. Hope	Pte

No. 1 Troop :

J. Bruce	Sgt
R. Barron	Sgt
L. Wickson	L/Sgt
R. Bellringer	L/Sgt
G. Hooper	Cpl
A. Smith	Cpl
J. Bishop	L/Cpl
A. Roussell	L/Cpl
B. Freeman	L/Cpl
W. Field	L/Cpl
E. Grief	L/Cpl
D. Cobelli	L/Cpl
L. Scully	Pte
W. Lawson	Pte
J. Newall	Pte

R. Amos	Pte
D. Salisbury	Pte
H. Anderton	Pte
V. Harding	Pte

No. 2 Troop :

E. Hewitt	TSM
L. Eldridge	Sgt
S. Hempstead	Sgt
L. Garland	L/Sgt
A. Maclare	L/Sgt
H. G. Taylor	Cpl
K. Patterson	L/Cpl
H. Garrett	L/Cpl
W. Heather	L/Cpl
R. O'Brien	L/Cpl
S. Stevenson	L/Cpl
H. Taylor	L/Cpl
R. Sims	L/Cpl
L. Chant	Pte
F. Evans	Pte
W. Grose	Pte
G. Lewis	Pte
H. Rowe	Pte
R. Thompson	Pte
G. Walton	Gdsmn

No. 3 Troop :

A. Maclean	Sgt

C. Davies	L/Sgt
L. Bayliss	L/Sgt
L. O'Donnell	Cpl
V. Finch	Cpl
A. Woodiwiss	Cpl
W. Beardsall	Cpl
J. Donaldson	L/Cpl
A. Howarth	L/Cpl
F. Thrift	L/Cpl
G. Ewens	L/Cpl
J. McDonald	Pte
W. Mattison	Pte
F. Gooch	Pte
J. Jarvis	Pte
J. Carroll	Pte
A. Elliott	Pte
J. Gardner	Pte
S. Holland	Pte
J. Dickenson	Pte
A. Sherwin	Pte
H. Simpson	Pte

No. 4 Troop :

T. Sherman	TSM
A. Wardle	Sgt
J. Gallagher	L/Sgt
J. Knowles	L/Sgt
E. Sinnott	Cpl
A. Rowe	L/Cpl
H. Mather	L/Cpl
J. Coughlan	L/Cpl
R. Cockin	L/Cpl
F. Parkes	L/Cpl
J. Fitchett	Pte
J. Maylott	Pte
D. Aird	Pte
J. Preston	Pte
S. Robinson	Gdsmn
W. Eckman	Pte
T. Diamond	Pte
W. Jones	Pte
H. Cunningham	Pte
F. Peachey	Pte
J. Fahy	Pte

No. 5 Troop :

| G. Haines | TSM |

W. Brown	Sgt
C. Jones	Sgt
D. Randall	L/Sgt
J. Rennie	L/Sgt
W. Challington	L/Sgt
J. Cheetham	Cpl
F. Holt	Cpl
W. Blythe	L/Cpl
E. Douglas	L/Cpl
R. Wilcox	L/Cpl
H. Roberts	L/Cpl
F. Sumner	L/Cpl
A. Ashcroft	Pte
W. Hughes	Pte
R. Milne	Gnr
J. McCormack	Pte
L. Wheelon	Pte
H. Cox	Pte
J. Gwynne	Pte
P. Honey	Pte
E. Hurst	Pte
F. Wilkes	Pte
S. Murdoch	Pte

No. 6 Troop :

S. Rodd	Sgt
H. Harrison	L/Sgt
W. Gibson	L/Sgt
P. Harkness	L/Sgt
J. Prescott	Cpl
N. Fisher	Cpl
R. Fursse	Cpl
R. M. Thomsett	Cpl
A. Young	L/Cpl
W. Dawson	L/Cpl
G. Hudson	L/Cpl
W. Watt	L/Cpl
R. Burns	L/Cpl
W. Spaul	L/Cpl
J. Cudby	Pte
F. Penfold	Pte
E. Tucker	Fus
G. Goss	Pte
A. Lucy	Pte
V. Woodman	Pte
W. Bell	Pte

P. Westlake	Pte
P. Bushe	Pte
G. Lloyd	Gdsmn
T. Roach	Pte

No. 1 Commando :

T. Durrant	Sgt
W. Chamberlain	L/Sgt
A. W. King	L/Sgt
R. Butler	L/Sgt
D. Chappell	L/Sgt
R. C. Bishop	Pte
E. Evans	Cpl
A. H. Dockerill	L/Sgt
F. Llewellyn	Cpl
E. Tomblin	Pte
A. Hopkins	Pte
G. Salisbury	Cpl

No. 2 Commando :

A. Mort	Cpl
G. Stanley	Cpl
J. Aldred	L/Cpl
J. Rogers	L/Cpl
J. Heery	L/Cpl
F. Holmes	Spr
R. Bradley	L/Sgt
G. Wheeler	Cpl
A. Peacock	L/Sgt
H. Fowler	L/Cpl
L. Homer	L/Cpl
A. Searson	L/Sgt

No. 3 Commando :

R. Brown	Cpl
S. Hailes	Tpr
F. Webb	L/Sgt
V. Coaker	L/Cpl
G. Churcher	L/Sgt
R. Jones	Cpl
E. Butler	L/Sgt
L. E. de la Torre	L/Cpl
G. Hudspeth	Spr
W. Day	L/Cpl
J. D. Boyd	Tpr
A. Nichols	L/Cpl

No. 4 Commando :

R. Bargman	L/Cpl
G. Coulson	Spr

No. 5 Commando :

G. Ide	Sgt
G. Bright	L/Sgt
L. Carr	Sgt
R. Beverridge	L/Sgt
W. Fergusson	L/Sgt
H. McKerr	L/Sgt
A. Howard	Cpl
W. Johnson	Bmbdr
G. Stokes	L/Cpl
D. Edwards	Pte
J. Brown	Pte
E. Johnson	Cpl

No. 9 Commando :

G. Hughes	L/Sgt
J. Deenes	Cpl
L. Burgess	L/Cpl
R. Duncan	L/Cpl
R. Jameson	Sgt
I. L. McLagan	Cpl
A. Walsham	Pte
B. Farquhar	Pte
J. Shenton	Pte
D. Richards	Pte
H. Shipton	Cpl
J. Apsden	L/Cpl

No. 12 Commando :

M. Deery	L/Sgt
S. Chetwynd	Cpl
A. Blount	Cpl
R. Wright	Cpl
T. Galloway	Cpl
J. Malloy	Cpl
R. Chung	Cpl
H. H. Jones	Cpl
J. Johnson	Cpl
F. Lemon	L/Cpl
J. Ferguson	Cpl
W. Reeves	Cpl
R. Hoyle	Cpl

No 2 Commando		L. Powell	Pte
Additional:		-. Walker	Pte
		T. Everitt	Pte
M. Shears	Pte	A. Neal	Pte
C. Fyfe	L/Cpl	E. Bryan	L/Cpl

BIBLIOGRAPHY

Butler, Rupert, *Hand of Steel*. Hamlyn Paperbacks, 1980
Flament, Marc, *Les Commandos*. Balland, Paris, 1972
Foot, M.R.D. & Langley, J.M., *M.I.9: Escape or Evasion 1939–45*.
  Futura, 1980
Holman, J. Gordon, *Commando Attack*. Hodder & Stoughton, 1942
Jones, Professor R.V., *Most Secret War*. Hamish Hamilton, 1978
Ladd, James, *Commandos and Rangers of World War II*.
  Macdonald & Jane, 1978
Lovat, Lord, *March Past*. Weidenfeld & Nicolson, 1978
Lucas Phillips, C.E., *The Greatest Raid of All*. Heinemann, 1958
Mason, David, *Raid on St Nazaire*. Macdonald & Co., 1970
Ryder, R.E.D., *The Attack on St Nazaire*. John Murray, 1947
Saunders, Hilary St George, *The Green Beret*. Michael Joseph, 1949
Young, Peter, *Commando*. Ballantine Books Inc., 1969
Combined Operations: The Official Story of the Commandos. Mac-
  millan, 1943
The Katyn Massacre: Crime of Katyn: Facts and Documents (of
  Katyn); report to House of Representatives, Washington, 19
  September 1950; report to Select Committee of US Congress in
  1951 by General Bissell. Report by Dr M. Wodzinski of the Polish
  Red Cross.

INDEX

Index